Faith Builders

Lisa Cooley Banks

Bankspraise Publishing
P.O. Box 1093
Grand Blanc, MI 48480

For conference or workshop scheduling contact Lisa at:
BPPublishing@yahoo.com

ISBN-13: 978-0578408521
ISBN-10: 057840852X

Unless otherwise indicated, all Scripture quotations are taken from the King James Version of the Bible.

Scripture quotations noted NKJV are taken from the New King James Version®. Copyright © 1982 by Thomas Nelson. Used by permission. All rights reserved.

Scripture quotations noted NIV are taken from the Holy Bible New International Version. Copyright © 1973, 1978, 1984, 2011 by Biblica, Inc.™ Used by Permission. All rights reserved worldwide.

Scripture quotations noted AMP are taken from AMPLIFIED Bible. Copyright © 1954, 1958, 1962, 1964, 1965, 1987 by the Lockman Foundation. All rights reserved. Used by permission. (www.Lockman.org)

CONTENTS

DEDICATION

First, I thank God for showing this little girl what a Father's love looks like. I also praise Him for the excellency of His grace that I accessed by faith.

To my husband, Rick, the love of my life: It is an honor to be your wife. Thanks for being a rock: solid, dependable and a fortress for our three and me.

To my favorite children, Brandon, Jamin, and Briana. You are proof of God's goodness to me. I am overjoyed at the privilege of being your mother. To Brandon, specifically, God told me to believe and after 12 years, I saw your face. I love you three to life!

To the three pastors who helped shape my love for learning the Word of God. The late Rev. Eugene Simpson, you introduced me to Christ. Pastor Tyrone Sweeney, you introduced me to the Holy Spirit and worship. My current Pastor Timothy R. Stokes, you introduced me to my purpose. I will be forever grateful for the role each of you played in my life. Pastor Stokes, you took the teacher in me to a whole 'nother level! You are an amazing 'potential-builder' and I love you dearly.

To my beautiful sister, Bernie Cooley Nelson, who went home to be with the Lord in the middle of my writing this book. God knew I needed this word to see me through your untimely home going, and my faith still looks up to Jesus who gives me grace. I refuse to sorrow like those who have no hope - I know where you are. See you later!

To my beautiful mother, the late Ellese Cooley, and the rest of my siblings, Elaine, Sondra, Pat, Joyce, Greg, my late brother Leon and that entire, humongous Cooley clan - people know us by our love! What a legacy our Mom left us! They say you can't pick your family, but if I could, I would still choose you.

To the Louisiana Banks crew, especially my Mother-in-love, Mineola Banks Jaggers. My children are blessed with two loving families and I am so grateful. I love you all.

To Pastor Tanya Stokes. I dedicate chapter 6 to you and your champion spirit. Your tireless stand in the face of adversity is inspiring to all who serve with you at Family Worship Center Church International. You are the epitome of Endurance.

To that gang of crazy praisers at Family Worship Center Church International. I love doing life and LIGHT with you. It feels so good to worship with those who constantly make a demand on the gift of God within you. #WeGetItFromOurPastor. Thank you for the encouragement and every single Amen (I see you Mary Calvin)!

To Beverly Towns, my friend and chief intercessor, who I feel at times has saved my life with her prayers. You, my dear, are simply priceless!

To Rochelle Wilson Ziyad. God used you to stoke the fires under the writer. Pen ready! Thanks for the blessing that you have been to me for years. You are one of a kind.

To my sister-friend Gloria Curry, who introduced me to a faith that caused me to believe on another level. I will always treasure our sisterhood and the words I heard when you ministered, "His Name is above Infertility!" It is indeed. I have the proof!

INTRODUCTION

The biggest spiritual battle of my life began when we first heard the word 'Infertility'. I come from a large family where I grew up with seven siblings and my husband's was even larger with eleven siblings and three additional step-siblings, not to mention the host of grandchildren. So hearing this word from the doctor didn't make sense in our world. Little did I know that God would use this challenge to teach me to fight with my faith, along with birthing in me an understanding of how faithful He is, and a passion to worship Him and provoke others to join me in His powerful, but loving presence.

I set out in this book to encourage others to trust Him and to return to the simplicity of faith in His Word. Know this – God always has a reward at the end of the fight!

So understanding faith is necessary if we are going to fight with it. We must believe in God and the principles of His Word in order to be saved and walk in the blessings of the kingdom of God that are promised to us as His children and joint heirs with His First-born Son, Jesus Christ.

The Apostle Paul tells us in Ephesians 2:8:

> *"For by grace are ye saved through faith; and that not of yourselves: [it is] the gift of God:"*

This grace is the unearned favor of God that releases salvation and other blessings to us. However, by God's design the only way to access His grace - His favor - is by believing in Him. What specifically are we to believe?

> *⁹That if thou shalt confess with thy mouth the Lord Jesus, and shalt believe in thine heart that God hath raised him from the dead, thou shalt be saved. ¹⁰For with the heart man believeth unto righteousness; and with the mouth confession is made unto salvation.*
> *Romans 10:9-10*

First and foremost, we must believe that God raised Jesus from the dead in order that we can be born again. Salvation – being born again - is the number one priority of our faith. Then in Hebrews we learn:

"But without faith [it is] impossible to please [him]: for he that cometh to God must believe that __He is__, and [that] __He is a rewarder__ of them that diligently seek him."
Hebrews 11:6

We must believe that God is God. We must come to believe that He alone is King of kings and Lord of lords, El Shaddai, the Almighty God. He alone is Omnipotent, Omniscient, and Omnipresent. And we must take it a step further and believe that He rewards us if we seek **HIM** with our whole hearts consistently. A rewarder is 'one who pays wages', which indicates that diligently seeking God in faith pays. So just as we expect a paycheck from our employers at the end of a work week, we should expect that our diligent pursuits to know God will pay off for us.

So, as you can see God is pretty big on trust: Notice that this same scripture tells us that without faith it is impossible to please Him. In this study we will focus on understanding how to do just that, by examining what faith is (and what it isn't), how to get faith and how to activate it in our lives so that we can become the people talked about in Hebrews 10:38, those who have been justified and now, "…live by faith."

So, grab your hard hats and let's get to building!

CONFIDENTIALITY NOTE

If you are using this as a group Bible study, then in addition to the weekly teachings to build your faith, this 7-week Bible study series includes small group discussion prompts designed to allow questions and answers as well as more personal ministry. The success of this format will require confidentiality among your group members: What's shared in the groups must remain in the groups. Please respect the process so that the others in your group feel free to share in confidence and can receive what God has for them.

LESSON 1
FAITH DEFINED

In many cases the Bible defines the words contained within scripture by context and comparison. However, in the case of the word *faith,* the writer of the book of Hebrews gives us a direct definition:

> Now **FAITH** is the **substance** of **things hoped** for, the **evidence** of **things not seen**.
>
> *Hebrews 11:1*

To clearly understand the fullness of this definition, it is necessary to look at the meaning and context of the words contained *in* it. Let's examine each word individually:

> **_NOW_**. Many Bible teachers have used this word '**_now_**' to support that faith means present tense. While faith does require that we believe God right now, this word is not the reason for this truth. According to Vine's Dictionary of New Testament Words (Vines), 'now' in this context, is merely a conjunction that means, '*moreover*', '*and*' or, *but*'.[1] This conjunction indicates that there is a connection between this passage and the one before it and requires that we look back to understand it in context. If we erroneously believe that it refers to a time marker, we will fail to look back for the connection between this passage and the previous one for a full contextual meaning.
>
> In the paragraphs before the writer says, "Now faith is," he was encouraging believers to stand fast in faith and not throw away their confidence because it carried a great reward. In verse 10:38 he said "Now the just shall live by faith," then in Hebrews 11:1 he uses 'now' to say 'moreover' here is what the faith that I just told you to live by really is. So again, while faith is always present tense, it is not because Hebrews 11:1 says, "Now faith."
>
> **_FAITH_**. The Hebrew (Old Testament) word for faith is "*emuwn*", meaning faithful, truth, faith.

The Greek (New Testament) word is *pistis,* and similarly refers to assurance, believe, belief, them that believe, fidelity. We will obviously take a closer look at this word throughout the series, but note here that 'fidelity' as a definition

**REMEMBER THIS:
NOW FAITH 'IS' THE SUBSTANCE
OF THINGS HOPED FOR, THE
EVIDENCE OF THINGS NOT SEEN.
HEBREWS 11:1**

hints that we are looking at the trustworthiness of the person we are trusting.

IS. This tiny two-letter word embodies the reason why faith means present tense. 'Is' is a form of the verb set 'to be' which indicates that something exists in the present tense. 'Was' is the past tense of that same verb set and 'will' is the future tense.

THE. This adjective is used as a definitive before nouns which are specific or understood; or it is used to limit their significance to a specific thing or things, or to describe them.

Okay so why define 'the'? Because it is important to understand that it is used to refer to a specific 'thing' not just something general, or one of many. It refers to something in particular. So faith is 'the' - not one of several – substances, and here it specifically refers to the substance of things hoped for.

Substance is a key component of the Biblical definition of faith because it is one of the two things Paul says 'faith is', therefore it's meaning is critical to our study.

SUBSTANCE. – *'hypostasis'* in the Greek, means, "a standing under, support", an "assurance" or "substance" which may signify a title-deed, as giving a guarantee, or reality. (Vines)

Thayer's Greek Lexicon (Thayer's) defines substance as "that which has foundation, is firm; hence

a. that which has actual existence; a substance, real being

I identify largely with the 'title-deed' definition because my husband and I are real estate investors. When I go to a property closing to finalize the deal on a purchase, I am given a title-deed signed by the seller indicating that I am now the owner of the property. This means that it does not matter who may currently physically occupy the property, I am now the owner and they have to vacate the premises or pay me rent, according to my instructions.

Substance says that my faith is a title-deed or guarantee, or reality of something – but of what? It is the substance of:

THINGS. HOPED FOR.

> ***THINGS***. Greek G4229 – pragma - Matter. That which is or exists. (Something real). Things can be tangible or intangible. It can be a better car, a house, tuition, peace in a crazy situation healing, restoration of your family or remedies for any number of situations that we face in life.

> ***HOPED FOR***. Greek G1679 – elpizo - in a Biblical sense, to *wait* for salvation with joy and full confidence.

> Webster's 1828 dictionary defines hope as, "A desire of some good, accompanied with at least a slight expectation of obtaining it, or a belief that it is obtainable."

I find this next part of the definition crucial in distinguishing hope from other related words.

> "Hope differs from wish and desire in this, that it implies some expectation of obtaining the good desired, or the possibility of possessing it. *Hope therefore always gives pleasure or joy; whereas wish and desire may produce or be accompanied with pain and anxiety."*[2]

So there appears to be three levels of believing here. Wishing, hoping and faith.

The writer has made a complete statement here, "Now, faith is the substance of things hoped for…" But just in case we didn't understand the first analogy, he says that our faith is also the evidence of things not seen.

> **_EVIDENCE_**. Greek G1650 – elegchos - a proof, that by which a thing is proved or tested. Conviction.

Evidence takes us into the legal system, where it represents **_proof_** that something presented before the judge proves a point in favor of either the plaintiff or the defendant.

But what is our faith evidence of?

> OF **_THINGS_**. Again, that which is or exists.

> **_NOT SEEN_**. Greek G991. Unable to see or discern with the physical eye.

So it is our faith in God's word that is proof that even though we cannot see whatever things we are praying for, they still belong to us.

Put it all together and define Faith in your own words. How do you see it?

_____

_____

_____

_____

Now let's look at some other defining points of faith.

What Faith Is – Believing is Seeing!

The Israelite patriarch Abraham is described in Romans 4 as the father of our faith.

*¹⁶Therefore [it is] of faith, that [it might be] by grace; to the end the promise might be sure to all the seed; not to that only which is of the law, but **to that also which is of the faith of Abraham;** who is **the father of us all,***

What did Abraham's faith look like, so that it was held up by God before us as a model of how to believe God? Let's look at Romans 4:18-21 to gain a glimpse.

*¹⁸Who **against hope believed in hope**, that he might become the father of many nations, **according to that which was spoken**, so shall thy seed be.*

*¹⁹And being not weak in faith, he **considered not his own body now dead**, when he was about an hundred years old, **neither yet the deadness of Sara's womb:***

*²⁰He **staggered not at the promise of God through unbelief;** but was strong in faith, **giving glory to God;***

*²¹And being **fully persuaded** that, **what he had promised, he was able also to perform.***

Let's look more closely.

1. First, Abraham ***hoped even though the situation appeared to be hopeless.*** He relied upon the promise of God and moved according to what was spoken to him by God. Abraham didn't give the natural circumstances priority over the Word of God, but began to focus on what God said would be. He didn't deny the circumstances. He just didn't let them override what God had said, and as a result he pleased God with actions that proclaimed that God is El Shaddai - the Almighty One. Abraham's faith message to us is this: Believing is seeing what God said and taking that as our reality.

2. Second, he ***did not stagger*** at the promise of God. This statement could be a little confusing at first if you have read

the Old Testament account of Abraham's life. It appeared that he did indeed waiver in his faith, trying to come up with his own solution. But what some see as contradiction in scripture always has a message of truth to real *Truth Seekers*. So using the context and comparison principles of Bible research to understand what is meant here, what we really see is a picture of a struggle in the fight of faith that Abraham endured and won!

In Genesis 15 we are introduced to the Abrahamic Covenant, where the patriarch questioned God about his heir, since he at this point had no children. After receiving the assurance from the Lord that the heir would be his natural son, born from his wife Sarah, verse 6 tells us "And he believed in the LORD; and He [the Lord] counted it to him for righteousness."

Then in chapter 16 we see the great compromise where Abraham conceded to his wife's request and slept with her maid, trying to manufacture their version of the promise since it was taking God too long to come through. Herein lies what appears to be a contradiction. But what we see instead is the mercy and grace of God, where God is really telling us that even through the ups and downs, as long as your faith makes it to the end of the race, you still win and He doesn't even consider that you had to fight doubt and unbelief to get there.

God only sees that we persevered in our fight of faith and ultimately and finally believed Him instead of the lies of the enemy. We need to remember this when we listen a little too long to the outside voices telling us something other than God's promises on the inside of us. This should encourage us that we are not backslidden, faithless, losers just because we listened to the enemy's voice. This is not an excuse to take the faith fight lightly, but an encouragement that when you do struggle in your believing, shake it off and get back on track like Abraham did, and watch God come through with your 'promised child.'

As long as we shake ourselves and snatch our minds back so that we do not let the doubt and unbelief settle into our spirits, then we are winning the fight of faith. The enemy likes to lure us into doubt, then turn around and accuse us of doubting, keeping us in a vicious cycle of 'No Confidence" and 'No Forward Progress!"

But he is a liar who has been exposed. Abraham's story teaches us that God only considers whether we believed him until the end. This is what gives glory to God. Did we endure to the end? Did we remind ourselves continually that God's word is the truth, the whole truth and nothing but the truth?

3. Third, we see the process of the fight of faith as we go through Abraham's story, and in the end, when all was said and done, he was ***fully persuaded*** that God was able to do what He promised. But his faith story doesn't end here. He had one more final test of faith.

   Finally, In Genesis 22, after receiving Isaac, his promised child, Abraham was instructed by God to literally offer him up as a sacrifice. Here we see what may be his greatest test of faith; his willingness to sacrifice that 'thing' for which he had waited so long. As he began the journey to the mountain to sacrifice Isaac, Abraham got to a certain point and in verse 5 told his servants to, "Stay here with the donkey while I and the boy go over there. We will worship and then ***we will come back*** to you." (NIV).

   This second account of Abraham's faith is so powerful that it is mentioned separately as a 'part 2' of Abraham's story in the Rollcall of Faith in Hebrews 11:19, stating that Abraham was *"…Accounting that God [was] able to raise [him] up, even from the dead; from whence also he received him in a figure."* Abraham's faith believed that even if Isaac's life was taken, ***God was not only able, but willing*** to raise him up from the dead.

So to recap, we see from Abraham's example that faith IS, hoping against hope, not staggering, fighting a good fight, and believing that God is able and God willing to do it for us.

We see another example of what faith is in Luke 7. Here, a centurion soldier came to Jesus asking for healing for one of his servants. Jesus was about to follow him home but this military leader made a profound statement in verses 6-9:

> ⁶*Lord, don't trouble yourself, for I do not deserve to have you come under my roof...* ⁷**say the word**, *and my servant will be healed.* ⁸*For* **I myself am a man under authority, with soldiers under me**. *I tell this one, 'Go,' and he goes; and that one, 'Come,' and he comes.* **I say to my servant, 'Do this,' and he does it."** ⁹*When Jesus heard this, he was amazed at him, and turning to the crowd following him, he said, "I tell you,* **I have not found such great faith even in Israel***."*

This centurion understood that the Words of Jesus were servants that carried authority and could be sent to do whatever He commanded them to do. Jesus' words still march like soldiers in battle to accomplish whatever He sends them to do in our lives as well. This centurion knew he didn't deserve for Jesus to respond to his request, but he took a leap of faith that Jesus would be merciful to him for his soldier's sake. He knew that Jesus' didn't have to come to his home, but that His Words carried enough power to do the job without him physically being there.

Jesus was amazed! That's saying a lot. He said he had never seen such great faith as this revelation of the power of His Words, even in Israel! So from this centurion's story we see that faith is believing that the Word is authorized to do what it has been sent to do, and as the prophet Isaiah said, it cannot return to God empty - short of accomplishing that which it has been sent to do. (Isa. 55:11)

What Faith Is Not! – Seeing is Believing

Another method of defining a word is to compare it to its opposite. Let's take a look now at what faith is not.

> *John 20:24-29 NIV*
> ²⁴*Now Thomas...one of the Twelve, was not with the disciples when Jesus came.* ²⁵*So the other disciples told him, "We have seen the Lord!" But he said to them, "**Unless I see** the nail marks in his*

*hands and put my finger where the nails were, and put my hand into his side, **I will not believe**." [26]A week later his disciples were in the house again, and Thomas was with them. Though the doors were locked, Jesus came and stood among them and said, "Peace be with you!" [27]Then he said to Thomas, "**Put your finger here; see my hands**. Reach out your hand and put it into my side. **Stop doubting and believe**." [28]Thomas said to him, "My Lord and my God!" [29]Then Jesus told him, "**Because you have seen me, you have believed; blessed are those who have not seen and yet have believed**."*

What do we see here that faith is not? It is not, waiting until we can see it with our own eyes or touch it with our hands, before we will believe. There is no faith required after you see something. Jesus did not commend this as faith, nor do we see Thomas mentioned in the *Rollcall of Faith* in Hebrews 11. Instead, Thomas, though he eventually believed, has gone down in history as what? "Doubting Thomas." People who do not even know the Bible will tell you not to be a "Doubting Thomas." Not because Thomas didn't ultimately believe, but because he didn't believe until he saw with his own physical eyes. That did not take faith.

Thomas' unbelief wouldn't allow him to reach beyond his physical senses into the spirit realm to believe that Jesus not only visited the other disciples, but that he was actually raised from the dead. Notice he didn't just say that he didn't believe Jesus came to visit them: He said until he saw the prints of the nails and thrust his hand into Jesus' side, he wouldn't believe. This sounds like he doubted Jesus' resurrection from the dead altogether. This is a message to us that if the Word says it, we need to reach beyond the natural circumstances and accept it into our hearts as truth.

Faith *is* also *not* mental assent, nor is it foolish or presumptive thinking.

Mental assent is believing with our head that God is real and the Bible is true. It is also reasoning that it could happen, but not really accepting it into our hearts and believing that it will happen for us. Notice here the difference in 'tenses' again. Mental assent is the predecessor of hope, but it can't stand on faith yet. It acknowledges the truth but not enough to believe that it will happen for us. Hebrews 11:6 tells us that we "...must believe that he [God] is, and [that] he is a rewarder of them that diligently seek him." We must not only believe that He is, but also that He will for us.

There are also those who claim to believe God, but walk in **foolishness** by 'claiming' things that scripture doesn't promise them nor is the will of God for them. They are not walking in the wisdom or will of God and appear to believe that God will contradict His Word to get something to them simply because they recite a few out-of-context scriptures and click their heels three times. This type of person usually hears what they want to hear from faith messages and goes off on a fleshly tangent to try to manipulate God, and his people, into doing something crazy for them. God will not be manipulated. We need to learn His Word and walk in it. When we stand in faith for what is guaranteed to us in the Word of God, then we can expect to see it. But throwing a few misplaced scriptures on a fleshly desire won't make it come to pass.

One example of this is that person who is *'believing'* God to bless them financially, but they won't look for a job. This is a contradiction of scripture as we see in 2nd Thessalonians 3:10 *"...this we commanded you, that if any would not work, neither should he eat."* Equally as foolish is someone believing God for a specific spouse when that person has no interest in them or may be 'espoused' to another. We will talk about the purpose of faith in the next lesson, but catch this hint...it is always about bringing glory to God and these antics only cause confusion and mock the Word of God.

Presumption is also not faith, but *"supposition of the truth or real existence of something, without direct or positive proof of the fact, but grounded on circumstantial or probable evidence which entitles it to belief."* (Webster's 1828). Related to faith, this necessarily means that we cannot stand on it, because it is does not have proof, which for us is faith in the Word of God. When we call ourselves standing in faith for something we want, when we have not sought God for whether or not it is His will for us, nor is it specifically

22

promised in scripture, we presume that God will grant it when in effect there is no covenant with God to do so.

An example of presumption would be hearing a good idea and running with it without asking God if it is His idea _for us_. It could be a good plan, but someone else's plan. A good idea is not always a God idea for us. The Psalmist David says, *"Delight thyself also in the LORD; and he shall give thee the desires of thine heart."* (Psalm 37:4) This first of all means God placing His desires in our hearts.

Those who presume in prayer usually lack a solid relationship with God but instead utter religious words and expect that because they followed some formula it will happen. Interestingly, presumption is also defined as behavior perceived as arrogant, disrespectful, and transgressing the limits of what is permitted or appropriate. The latter part of this definition identifies the spirit of this counterfeit *faith*. People walking in presumption are often pompous about their 'things.'

Other Key Scriptures Defining Faith

Another key scripture passage that helps us to define faith and begin to understand how it works is Mark 11:22-24.

> [22]*"Have faith in God," Jesus answered.* [23]*"Truly I tell you, if anyone says ...and does not doubt in their heart but believes that what they say will happen, it will be done for them.* [24]*Therefore I tell you, whatever you ask for in prayer, believe that you have received it, and it will be yours. (NIV)*

Here Jesus is telling His disciples to have faith in God. He then goes on to show them what walking in faith looks like. There are several key components of faith seen here that cannot be ignored even though modern society often mocks the simplicity of the instructions Jesus gave.

The first key here is Jesus telling them that something must be spoken. He told them that whoever

> *SAYS*. And does
> NOT DOUBT in his heart. But

23

BELIEVES that those
THINGS (those *'things'* again!), which he
SAYS shall happen, it will.

He tells us that Whatever we ask for,
when we **pray** (*SAY*), if we
BELIEVE that we receive it
then it will be ours.

These passages emphasize the principle of believing that we receive what we ask God for *when* we pray. We trust that *as we speak* the words to God that the things have gone from being something we hope will happen in the future to something that, even though I may not see it with my natural eyes right now, the title deed has been transferred to me and it is legally mine!

If you have purchased a home or vehicle you will understand this principle. After signing the paperwork with the seller you are given a title deed indicating that ownership has been transferred from them to you. Especially with a house; you don't necessarily take possession of it that same day, but it is legally yours and the courts will work with you to force whoever is occupying it to get out and hand it over to you. As a matter of fact, if the sellers are still in the house the next day, they are required to pay you rent until they leave.

So what is the title deed that proves that we own what we have faith for? **Faith** in the **Word of God** is our title deed. To move from hope to faith we must find scriptures to stand on in the same way that Jesus used the Word when He was tempted of the devil. Each time satan presented Jesus with an alternative to God's will for Him, Jesus responded, "It is written." If it worked for Jesus, it will work for us! When we believe as we pray, we receive the title deed and legal ownership becomes ours. Anyone trying to deny our possession of it must then be taken to the court of the Word of God to be dealt with.

FAITH IS DOING

The last defining point in our definition of faith is action. There are several scriptures that deal with this ingredient. James the brother of Jesus tells us that,

"But wilt thou know, O vain man, that faith without works is dead?"

James 2:20

This is a confirmation of every instance in the New Testament where faith was being used for a miracle. The person receiving the miracle had to get up and act like they had received it. Consider the example from Luke 5 where the friends of a man with the palsy lifted him up to the rooftop because of the crowd, dug a hole and lowered him down to get an audience with Jesus. Verse 20 says,

> *"And when he <u>saw their faith</u>, he said unto him, Man, thy sins are forgiven thee."*

But the healing was not manifested yet. After a religious back and forth with the Pharisees concerning whether or not Jesus had the power to heal, he resolved it by speaking again to the man with the palsy saying,

> *[24]" ...<u>Arise, and take up thy couch</u>, and go into thine house. [25]And <u>immediately he rose up before them</u>, and <u>took up that whereon he lay</u>, and <u>departed to his own house</u>, glorifying God."*

At the point of Jesus telling him to get up, there was no evidence of his healing. He had to believe he was healed or he would not have even made the attempt to get up off his bed.

Also consider the story of the woman with the issue of blood, who said in Mark 5:27-28:

> *[27]"... When she had heard of Jesus, came in the press behind, and touched his garment. [28]For <u>she said, If I may touch</u> but his clothes, I shall be whole."*

In these stories and many more throughout the New Testament we see that the recipients began to act on what they believed. The man's friends believed that if they could just get him to Jesus he would be whole, so they got up and busted up somebody else's roof in faith. The woman, in faith, believed that if she could just touch Jesus' garment she would be whole, so she defied the traditions of the day that said she should be somewhere in hiding, and reached out to touch Jesus.

Building My Faith

What is written concerning what *you* are hoping for? We must learn to meditate on the Word of God – the language in that title deed that promises what we are hoping for - as our faith develops for that thing. Romans 10:17 tells us that "…faith comes by hearing and hearing by the Word of God." We begin by identifying that thing that we are hoping for. We continue to confess the Word until it becomes one with our spirit and we are no longer hoping that it will happen, but we instead reach the point of believing that it is indeed ours, moving us from hope to faith. In Lesson 4 there is a *Hope to Faith Worksheet* that will walk you through this process. I challenge you now to begin to think about those things that you have given up on, take them off the 'it will never happen for me' shelf and begin to ask God if that is His will for you.

Lesson 1 Reflections:

1. Write out the key scripture that literally defines Faith?

2. What is the difference between faith and hope?

3. How can something invisible be 'substance' and 'evidence'?

4. What three things does Abraham's story teach us that faith looks like?

5. What does Abraham's example teach us about doubt and staggering?

6. How does the devil use doubt?

7. What is mental assent?

8. What two things must we believe about God in order to please Him?

9. What do our words have to do with our faith?

10. How do we know we believe?

Journey from Hope to Faith Worksheet

I Hope:

The Words in my Title Deed:

    Scripture 1.

    Scripture 2.

    Scripture 3.

My confession: (Write out what you believe about your situation based upon the scriptures you wrote above.)

LESSON 2
THE PURPOSE OF FAITH

The late Myles Munroe spent a great deal of his ministry focusing on the 'purpose of a thing,' noting many times that if we don't understand it we will abuse it. We have seen this happen in the body of Christ in the area of faith where 'believers' abused the principles of faith in ignorance and as a result often brought a reproach on the name of God instead of bringing glory to Him. We want to set forth the purpose of faith so that we can properly live that life of faith that the *just* – those who have been justified and declared righteous - are instructed to live.

FAITH FOR GRACE FOR SALVATION

That being said, the Bible, in passages like Romans 10:9-10, makes it clear that the primary object of our faith is grace – the unearned favor of God; and the primary purpose of faith is then that we might believe for the grace that brings salvation.

> [9]*That if thou shalt confess with thy mouth the Lord Jesus, and shalt <u>believe</u> <u>in thine heart</u> that God hath <u>raised him from the dead</u>, <u>thou shalt be saved</u>. [10]For with the heart man believeth unto righteousness; and with the mouth confession is made unto <u>salvation</u>.*

But what exactly is salvation? A lot of people believe that this means you have gone to an altar and joined a church. That is not half the truth. Consider the Biblical meaning laid out in *Outline of Biblical Usage* by Larry Pierce[1]:

I.   Greek = soteria = deliverance, preservation, safety, salvation

1. deliverance from the molestation of enemies
2. … that which concludes to the soul's safety
3. salvation as the present possession of all true Christians
4. future salvation, the sum of benefits and blessings which the Christians, redeemed from all earthly ills, will enjoy after the visible return of Christ from heaven in the…eternal kingdom of God.

We see salvation here mentioned in three different time dimensions – 1) past, 2) present and 3) future.

1. Past – The first phase of salvation is described as being delivered from the molestation of the enemy. When we accept Christ as our Savior, satan is no longer our lord, and has no authority to molest - disturb or annoy us anymore. Salvation in effect restores us to right relationship with God, the true definition of righteousness. This restoration process reconciles us back to the good graces of our loving Father and Creator, giving us access to Him by our faith in the resurrection of our Lord Jesus Christ.

Why does it take Faith to be reconciled to God? As mentioned in the introduction, trust is a big deal to God. But why is faith required for fixing the problem from the garden of Eden? The reason is simple. The lack of faith is what caused the problem in the first place. Remember that God told Adam and Eve not to eat of the fruit of the tree of the knowledge of good and evil. Eve listened to God's enemy, then began to doubt God's word. This treasonous offense is what opened the door for the fall. She and Adam chose to believe the lie of the enemy of God instead of the Word of their loving Creator. So in order to have our place back, we have to return our allegiance back to God by returning our trust to Him from the god of this world.

In Genesis 3 we see the death sentence pronounced upon mankind. But John 3:16 tells us that eternal life is again available to those who *believe* in the Son of God. However, John 3:18 also informs us that whoever does not believe is damned. We see confirmation in Romans 10:9 as quoted earlier that believing, or faith, is required for salvation.

> *⁹That if thou shalt confess with thy mouth the Lord Jesus, and shalt <u>believe in thine heart</u> that God hath raised him from the dead, <u>thou shalt be saved</u>.*

Salvation in the past tense simply means that once we have *believed* in our hearts and *confessed* with our mouths that Jesus is the Son of God and that God has raised Him from the dead (Rom. 10:9-10) we have *accepted* Jesus Christ as our Savior. We *have **been*** born again. Our spirits have ***been*** made new. Paul, in I Corinthians 5:17 confirms that,

"...if any man [be] in Christ, [he is] a new creature: old things are passed away; behold, all things are become new."

Once this happens, it is a done deal – history - but we must now learn to walk in newness of life, working out our soul's salvation with fear and trembling.

> 2. Present – The second phase of salvation is seen in the saving of our souls – our minds, wills and emotions - in the present tense, the Holy Spirit working in us to transform us into the image of Christ.

> *[12]Wherefore, my beloved, as ye have always obeyed, not as in my presence only, but now much more in my absence, work out your own salvation with fear and trembling. [13]For it is God which worketh in you both to will and to do of [his] good pleasure.*
> *Philippians 2:12-13*

The Apostle is telling us a few things here. First, working out the salvation of our souls requires that we walk in obedience to the Word, not only when we are in the presence of spiritual leadership, but even behind closed doors. We are to fear and respect God enough to walk in obedience to His Word.

Second, we see in verse 13 a connection between this phase of salvation and faith in the fact that it is God working in us to do His will and His good pleasure. And remember that Hebrews 11:6 tells us that without faith it is impossible to please God.

While it takes faith to be saved on all three levels, the most regularly active part of our faith is in being transformed into the image of Jesus Christ, which involves a daily walk making decision after decision to trust that He knows what is best for us in the face of situations where our natural minds have been trained to do something different. This is why Paul told us to:

"...be not conformed to this world: but be ye transformed by the renewing of your mind, that ye may prove what [is] that good, and acceptable, and perfect, will of God."

Romans 12:2

Brainwashing mostly carries a negative connotation, but in the case of renewing our minds, we want to be brainwashed. Consistent study and meditation on the Word of God is so important to being successful in working out our soul salvation. This is what renews our minds – the Word! We want the washing of the water of the Word that is talked about in Ephesians 2:26; the means by which Christ will sanctify us so that He can present to Himself a glorious church without spot, wrinkle, blemish or any such thing. Washing our thoughts causes us to think like He thinks, see like He sees, hear like He hears and act like He would act if He were here in the flesh. Remember we are His body and we should respond to the commands from our Head, who is Christ Jesus.

How do we practically work out our soul salvation? Paul says with 'fear and trembling' because God's Word requires that we live above the standards of this world. Our natural mindset, because of the worldview that most of us grew up with, is to manifest the works of the flesh. However, once we have been born again, we have to work to renew our minds so that we manifest the fruit of God's spirit. This takes faith because we have been trained to believe that the fleshly way is 'normal' and furthermore it is what the world expects. So we face rejection and ridicule when we separate ourselves from their philosophies and begin to do things God's way. But we must fear the consequences of displeasing God more than we fear being rejected by man. As the Apostle Peter said in Acts 5:29, "...we ought to obey God rather than men." We learn to meditate on the Word of God which again cleanses our minds from what this world has taught us, and builds within us the courage to trust and obey Him.

Equally as important is changing our hearts to desire God's results and not what we have been conditioned to think should be. For example, if somebody hurts you, the normal reaction is to get them back otherwise you look weak. It takes faith to step away from what you believed and did before you received Christ, and to trust that God's 'different' way will get better results; walking away and trusting that if we bless our enemies and those that despitefully use us, God will make things right for us.

What does this soul salvation look like?

Several passages speak to what our new life in Christ should look like as we begin to walk in newness of life, but Paul's letter to the Romans is the most complete explanation on the doctrine of faith as being a life lived by the spirit. Chapter 8 in particular speaks of life in the Spirit as compared to a life that tries to please God just by doing good deeds in our 'un-renewed' state. We are warned against trying to please God by ourselves before being born again, as no man can do so. Romans 8:14 tells us that as sons (daughters) of God we are to be led by the Spirit of God.

In Galatians 5, Paul lays out what the fruit of this Spirit-led life should look like but it first tells us what following our flesh will produce.

> [16]*[This] I say then, walk in the Spirit, and ye shall not fulfil the lust of the flesh.* [17]*For the flesh lusteth against the Spirit, and the Spirit against the flesh: and these are contrary the one to the other: so that ye cannot do the things that ye would.* [18]*But if ye be led of the Spirit, ye are not under the law.*

> [19]*Now the works of the flesh are manifest, which are [these]; Adultery, fornication, uncleanness, lasciviousness,* [20]*Idolatry, witchcraft, hatred, variance, emulations, wrath, strife, seditions, heresies,* [21]*Envyings, murders, drunkenness, revellings, and such like: of the which I tell you before, as I have also told [you] in time past, that they which do such things shall not inherit the kingdom of God.*

> [22]*But the fruit of the Spirit is love, joy, peace, longsuffering, gentleness, goodness, faith,* [23]*Meekness, temperance: against such there is no*

law. ²⁴And they that are Christ's have crucified the flesh with the affections and lusts. ²⁵If we live in the Spirit, let us also walk in the Spirit. ²⁶Let us not be desirous of vain glory, provoking one another, envying one another.

As believers we have to take on a mindset of victory and stop saying what we cannot do; stop justifying the weakness of our flesh by saying that a certain trait of sin "just runs in my family", or 'that's just how we are.' We must realize that we have been bought with a price and we have the same power of God that raised Jesus Christ from the dead living on the inside of us. (Eph. 1:19)

Our faith in His grace – or empowerment – is enough to lift us out of the darkness of our weaknesses into His marvelous Light! Go ahead and believe for the victory that has been won for you in Christ Jesus! It is yours! Own it!

3. Future – The final phase of salvation will take place in our bodies at the second coming of Jesus Christ. The *second* phase is a preparation for the 'rapture' as it is commonly referred to, where Jesus is preparing His bride to be presented to Himself. Matthew 10:22 tells us that "…he that endureth to the end *shall be* saved." He that fights the good fight of faith and does not abandon the Word of God for the cares of this life will meet Jesus in the sky on that great day.

FAITH TO FULFILL OUR CALLING

The second priority of our faith is the grace necessary to fulfill our calling. Believers who are not called to one of the five-fold ministry gifts often do not recognize that they were created by God's design to carry out an assignment in the earth. In other words, we all have a calling and it is fulfilling this calling that brings glory to God from our lives. Some are called to be healers in the medical industry, some to fight for justice in the legal profession, some to build wealth for His Kingdom in the business arena. Some are called to receive and carry out knowledge of witty inventions.

Our top motivational gifts as described in Romans 12:6-8 are clues to what God's callings on our lives are. If you have any question about your calling or purpose in life, study these seven gifts and pray that God will begin to reveal to you His calling on your life. It is there, and when you begin to develop and operate in it you will begin to bring glory to God in ways you never imagined possible. There is an excellent resource by Don and Katie Fortune, that includes a test to help you "*Discover Your God-Given Gifts.²*"

In addition to these callings it is every believer's call to be an ambassador for Christ, sharing the good news of God's love for all of mankind. Jesus' last message to his disciples as recorded in Matthew 28, was a reminder to them of who He is, and therefore who they are and what they are to do.

> *¹⁸And Jesus came and spake unto them, saying, __All power is given unto me__ in heaven and in earth.*
>
> *¹⁹__Go ye therefore__, and teach all nations, baptizing them in the name of the Father, and of the Son, and of the Holy Ghost:*
>
> *²⁰Teaching them to observe all things whatsoever I have commanded you: and, lo, I am with you alway, [even] unto the end of the world. Amen.*

As the body of Christ, we are what He is and have what He has, enabling us to do what He created us to do. All power was given unto Jesus, but then He tells us to "Go, therefore!" According to Paul, in II Cor. 5:20, we are "…ambassadors for Christ." Ambassadors represent the country they are from in a foreign land. Our new birth, when we accept Jesus as our Savior, means that our old man is dead and we are no longer of, or from, this world, but of, or from, the Kingdom of God.

A few verses earlier, in this same chapter Paul talked about us being reconciled back to God. We don't belong to this world anymore and we are not governed by its 'laws' and mindsets. (This doesn't mean we are not obligated to obey the laws of this land, but the laws of the

Kingdom of God supersede the laws of this world, and if there is any conflict between the two, God's Word prevails in our hearts and lives even to the point of our being willing to suffer or even die in obedience to it.)

FAITH FOR 'THINGS'

Salvation also includes being made whole again and to get a full picture of that, we need to revisit the garden to see what we were supposed to have in the first place. Regarding the creation of man, we find the following account in Genesis 1:

> [26]*And **God said**, Let us **make man in our image**, after our **likeness**: and **let them have dominion** over the fish of the sea, and over the fowl of the air, and over the cattle, and over all the earth, and over every creeping thing that creepeth upon the earth.*
>
> [27]*So **God created** man in his [own] image, in the image of God created he him; male and female created he them. [28]And **God blessed them**, and God said unto them, be **fruitful**, and **multiply**, and **replenish** the earth, and **subdue** it: and **have dominion** over the fish of the sea, and over the fowl of the air, and **over every living thing that moveth upon the earth**.*
>
> *Genesis 1:26-28*

Man was not subject to anything God made, only to God Himself. Adam and Eve were 'large and in charge' of everything God made and given instructions *and* empowerment to carry out their assignment to be fruitful, multiply and replenish the earth. This is the foundation for believing God for 'things' and is absolutely scriptural as well, when taken in context with the whole of scripture. This aspect of the definition of salvation refers to wholeness including health and wealth as we call it today.

The Apostle Matthew provides another important point on believing God for 'things.'

31 Therefore take no thought, saying, What shall we eat? or, What shall we drink? or, Wherewithal shall we be clothed?

32 (For after all these things do the Gentiles seek:) for your heavenly Father knoweth that ye have need of all these things.

33 But seek ye first the kingdom of God, and his righteousness; and all these things shall be added unto you.

34 Take therefore no thought for the morrow: for the morrow shall take thought for the things of itself. Sufficient unto the day [is] the evil thereof.
Matt. 6:31-34

As mentioned, there has definitely been misuse of scripture with people 'believing' God in what the world likes to call the 'name it, claim it' move. But as believers we cannot allow the world to intimidate us and cause to shrink back into fear, unwilling and unable to speak His Word for what He has promised. We should still live in expectation that He will move on our behalf even with regards to material possessions.

We have every right as His sons and daughters to ask God for healing, new homes and new cars and other material blessings, but we must do so with the right spirit and according to His Word. Consider the Psalmist David's words in Psalm 37:

1 ... Do not fret because of evildoers, Nor be envious of the workers of iniquity.

3 Trust in the LORD, and do good; Dwell in the land, and feed on His faithfulness.

4 Delight yourself also in the LORD, And He shall give you the desires of your heart.

⁵Commit your way to the LORD, Trust also in Him, And He shall bring [it] to pass. ...

⁶And he shall bring forth thy righteousness as the light, and thy judgment as the noonday.

⁷Rest in the LORD, and wait patiently for Him; <u>Do not fret because of him who prospers in his way</u>, Because of the man who brings wicked schemes to pass.

David gives us perspective here. Oftentimes we allow the world to dictate what 'things' we want, based on what we observe those around us getting. Matthew says that we are to seek God's kingdom first and even more importantly, David says we are to allow God to place His desires in our hearts. If we are truly seeking Him, then we expect a divine exchange of His thoughts for our thoughts and His ways for our ways. The things around us are not as important to us as seeing His Kingdom agenda carried out. The amazing thing about God is that when we are not focused on the 'things' but His will, He actually blesses us with those things because He can trust us to use them to do His will.

As Paul said in II Cor. 9:10, God gives seed to the sower. He blesses those who will use those blessings to minister to others. so we do not fret because of what others have, but we also do not fear wealth because of the opinion of unbelievers regarding what we should and should not have as Christians. They want us to take a vow of poverty, but they won't. They are okay with ungodly celebrities and athletes having wealth, but want those who are naming the name of Jesus Christ to live modestly. This is deception designed to stifle evangelism and minimize the growth of the Kingdom of God. They do not get that much input in my life and I challenge you to keep them out of your financial business. I am not for ministries who misuse finances, but I also do not let their abuses stop me from prospering. I believe that I am supposed to have more than enough, because I cheerfully support the Kingdom of God and give generously to others. If I do not have it, I cannot give it.

40

Our God is a loving Father who desires that His children have good things, but most important is His will, His master plan being carried out in the earth. While we cannot become overwhelmed with desire for things in this life, we can expect that our Father will bless us and prosper us even as our souls prosper.

In summary, we see that our priority in faith is to access the grace, the unearned favor of God for: Salvation; Allowing Christ to be conformed in us; Carrying out our God-given assignment and sharing Christ with others; and Reclaiming our wholeness including whatever material needs (those other 'things') are required to fulfill our purpose. They'll be added, too. Without faith, try as hard as we may, we cannot access grace for anything from God, nor can we in our frail human attempts please God.

Reflections:

1. What is the real object of our faith? Explain.

2. What is the most important purpose for our faith?

3. What is the Greek word for salvation and what does it mean?

4. What are the three phases of salvation and which one are we in now?

5. How do we practically work out our soul salvation?

6. Identify an area where you are struggling in your flesh.

7. What scriptures can you meditate on as your work out your salvation in this area?

8. What do you feel is God's calling on your life? Your purpose?

9. What 'help' do you need from God to carry out this purpose?

10. What scriptures can you stand on to believe for the help you need to carry out God's will for your life?

11. In addition to our individual calling from God, what is every believer called to do? Provide scripture support for your answer.

12. Where do you think most of your desires come from (for real…not a religious answer here)?

13. When is it okay to ask God for 'things'?

14. Explain what being an ambassador is?

15. What are the three primary purposes for our faith as discussed in this lesson?

LESSON 3
HOW FAITH COMES

In lessons 1 and 2 we defined faith and discussed how we cannot access God nor His grace without it. We saw also where Paul told us in Hebrews 11:6 that we cannot please God without it. The late Kenneth E. Hagin, in *Faith Bible Study*, had the following to say regarding faith and pleasing God.

> *"If God demands that I have faith when it is impossible for me to have faith, then I have a right to challenge His justice. But if He places within my hands the means whereby faith can be produced, then the responsibility rests with me whether or not I have faith."[1]*

His statement speaks to the **just** or **fair** nature of the character of God, who would not require something of us that is not possible. Since faith is required, it must be possible to obtain it. So now we explore the question of just how to get it. We have two key scriptures to review as we look for an answer.

> **³For I say, through the grace given unto me, to every man that is among you, not to think [of himself] more highly than he ought to think; but to think soberly, according as God hath dealt to every man the measure of faith.**
>
> **Rom 12:3**

> **¹⁷So then faith [cometh] by hearing, and hearing by the word of God.**
>
> **Romans 10:17**

1. WE ARE GIVEN A MEASURE OF FAITH

We see first of all in Romans 12:3 that God has already dealt to every man a measure of faith, people just often don't recognize that it is faith. But if you stop and think about it, everybody trusts things and people and processes every single day. As a matter of fact, if someone doesn't walk in what society considers normal levels of trust, they are said to have an anxiety disorder, because it is not normal to distrust everything and everybody.

So we have faith, we just have to be careful where we place it. In the natural, we have faith that when we sit in a chair it is going to hold us and not collapse upon contact. We expect that when we put in forty hours at our jobs, at the end of the week there will be a paycheck. We in Michigan expect that when September comes, the leaves will change colors and fall from the trees and the skies a few months later will give way to snowy winters. We have been conditioned by our experiences to trust that these things will happen. All of these are examples of faith in our natural circumstances and environment. In Psalm 19:1, David tells us that the heavens declare the glory of God, giving us a glimpse of his handiwork that we come to trust in daily. We have been dealt a measure of faith so that we trust enough to function in our natural world.

In the preceding verses in Romans 12, we find Paul admonishing us to present our bodies to God as a living sacrifice, holy and acceptable unto Him and then he indicates that this is just a reasonable service. Paul here is dealing more with the matter of our soul's salvation as discussed in lesson 2. Presenting our bodies is a decision of our will which must be under the control of the Holy Spirit in order for us to accomplish this. Well how are we able to do this? Because God has dealt to us a measure of faith, the capacity for faith, upon which to build our lives. You have to have a little to start, that spark of hope watered with the Word that if cultivated will blossom into believing that God will do 'that' for you. So everyone is dealt enough faith to believe for salvation; we just have to choose to place our faith in the saving grace of Jesus Christ and not some counterfeit.

2. <u>WE INCREASE OUR FAITH BY HEARING THE WORD OF GOD.</u>

The second reference to how we get faith is probably the most popular scripture on the subject. We see in Romans 10:17 that faith in God comes to us by a certain God-prescribed method – hearing. And not just hearing anything, but hearing the Word of God. Let's first explore hearing as a natural physical sense.

Obviously, hearing is one of the five physical senses that represents a complex process of picking up sound and attaching meaning to it. Just as hearing is crucial to understanding the natural world around us, hearing spiritually is critical to understanding and finding our way in the spiritual realm.

Our human ears respond to the sounds they hear, sounds that can be very faint or very loud. Webster Dictionary's definition of hearing informs us that "even before birth, infants respond to sound." The ear has three primary sections that lead to the brain – the outer, middle and inner ear. In the natural, the sound of words is funneled down through our outer ears into our ear canals, striking our eardrums and causing vibration, a shaking that in turn creates the fluid in our inner ear to move in a way that transmits electrical signals from the inner ear to the auditory nerve to the brain for translation.[2]

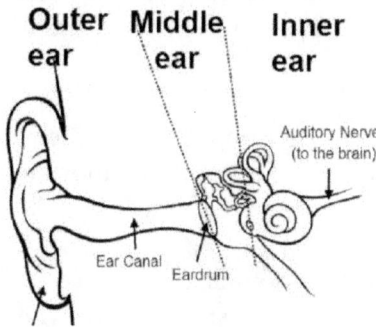

When we hear the Word of God initially there is a new sound that our brains have to process. The shaking that takes place has to ultimately be interpreted by our brains, which gives us our cues as to what to do with this new sound. Interestingly, the more we hear that sound, the more familiar we become with it and the more likely we are to yield to it, welcoming it to give direction to our lives. So it is with God's Word: Hearing it consistently reinforces its power to work in our lives because we are more likely to yield to it the more we hear it.

The Greek words, 'logos' and 'rhema' are both translated 'word' in the New Testament, both meaning basically 'that which has been uttered by a living voice.' Ephesians 6:17, however begins to point to a difference between the two; a difference that underscores the need to fill ourselves with the Word of God.

Vines Expository Dictionary of New Testament has the following to say about the distinction between logos and rhema,

> *The significance of 'rhema' (as distinct from 'logos') is exemplified in the injunction to take "the sword of the Spirit, which is the word of God," (Eph. 6:17) where the reference is not to the whole Bible*

as such, but to the individual scripture which the Spirit brings to our remembrance for use in time of need, a prerequisite being the regular storing of the mind with Scripture.[3]

As I have heard said through the years, the Holy Spirit can't bring back to your remembrance something that you never remembered in the first place. It is crucial to study the word of God so that when situations arise, the Holy Spirit can remind us of what God's Word says. This becomes the choice sword for the fight we find ourselves in at the time; that 2-edged sword that defeats the enemy of the Word of God every single time.

I remember as my children were growing up I taught them to say confessions from the Word of God as we started each morning. The opening lines said,

"I am a Banks and I dominate.
Any obstacle that comes before me must bow before me.
Jesus is Lord over my spirit, my soul and my body.
I can do all things through Christ who strengthens me."

My oldest son Brandon is a gifted speaker and was sent to represent his school at a regional oratorical contest. He had practiced diligently but when we sat to listen to the first contestants in his category he was a bit unnerved at how good they were (…and they were REAAALLY GOOD!) There was a break before his presentation and he approached me wide-eyed and I could smell the fear. I looked in his eyes and said, "Who are you?" He didn't even hesitate. What was in him came out. He said, "I am a Banks and I dominate!" And he did…He won and it wasn't even close!

'WHAT' You Hear Is Key

So the physical support for why faith comes by continuously hearing, is supported even in the science of hearing as it is a constant bombardment on our brains of words filled with suggestions, guidance, and encouragement to move in the direction of God's will for our lives. And as Paul indicates in the second phrase, we must also understand that it is WHAT we hear that is crucial. He says, "…hearing by the Word of God."

Faith is built by hearing God's Word, God's Voice, and allowing no other voice to overtake the place of authority in our hearts. Ancient, as well as modern religious doctrine must yield to the Word of God. Man's new age ideology and popular opinion must yield to the Word of God. In our modern twentieth-first century society, talk shows have become quite popular; talk shows where opinions about everything under the sun are broadcasted. Internet access has also opened up opportunities for countless people to announce their varying opinions on every aspect of life. As believers we can feel the temptation to lay aside our 'ancient and outdated' beliefs and join modern societal thinking, but we must never surrender our stance that **God's Word is unchangeable** just as He is. He never changes nor does His Word. That is the absolute undergirding of our being able to trust His Word. It is not situational, seasonal nor subject to the whims of time or circumstance. God's Words will never pass away!

FEAR ALSO COMES BY HEARING. As Paul instructs that faith comes by hearing, understand also that the same is true for fear. Fear is really just another form of faith, only faith in the negative. This is why the second phrase in Romans 10:17 is so important and where too many people miss it. *What* we hear will determine whether we walk in faith or fear. If we hear the Word of God, then we will build our faith. If we listen to the voice of God's enemy, then like Adam and Eve we will eventually succumb to his misleading and trust his temporary solutions instead of standing fast on the Word of God. Therefore, it is critical that we make constant, continuous hearing of the Word of God a regular part of our daily lives. We must take in God's word more than we listen to other views of life. And if we truly trust the words of God, we must listen with the intent of obeying them.

Really Hearing:

We have explored the natural aspect of hearing, but obviously hearing with the natural ears alone is not enough or everyone would be saved, and walking in victory. Hearing, in the Old Testament Hebrew had a much deeper meaning than the words translated from the Greek. '*Shama*', the Hebrew word for hearing as seen in Exodus 24:7, actually means to be obedient, signifying that you have listened and really HEARD with the intention of obeying the Word you heard. That is hearing! Hearing 'under' authority. Hearing as if you are a servant to the words, and bow in submission to their place of authority in your life. Not just receiving audible sounds, but paying attention to what's said and acting on it. That is hearing!

This truth is supported by the biological brother of Jesus in James 1:22-25 where James tells us,

> *²²But be ye doers of the word, and not hearers only, deceiving your own selves.*
> *²³For if any be a hearer of the word, and not a doer, he is like unto a man beholding his natural face in a glass:*
> *²⁴For he beholdeth himself, and goeth his way, and straightway forgetteth what manner of man he was.*
> *²⁵But whoso looketh into the perfect law of liberty, and continueth [therein], he being not a forgetful hearer, but a doer of the work, this man shall be blessed in his deed.*

Imagine James' perspective. He grew up watching his big brother Jesus, then after His death on the cross began to remember and reconsider everything he saw and heard him do. After losing a relative to death it is natural to remember every way they responded to the simple things in life as we begin to experience those events without them. After my mother passed away, her words rang even louder in my memory as I carried out the simplest of daily routines. Again after experiencing my sister's transition to be with the Lord, I am already hearing her in my heart, saying things (sometimes the little quirky things) to which I did not pay as much attention before. Actually, after she passed, most of us began immediately overusing the word 'What-Ever!' in her sassy tone.

So James had a unique perspective. As a child he watched Jesus' life and character being built like no one else, probably not realizing the significance of what he was experiencing until much later in his life after his big brother was gone from the earth. James tells us from this vantage point that the key to getting our prayers answered by God, is doing what the Word says after we hear it, as a sign that we have truly heard 'under.'

There are many stories in scripture where people heard the Word, believed and acted on it. That is when they saw God move because of their faith. Consider the account in Acts 14:7-10 where the lame man who was crippled from birth **HEARD** Paul speak, then had faith to be healed **and responded** to Paul's instruction to," *...Stand upright on thy feet. And he leaped and walked."*

One of my favorite stories of healing in the Bible is of the woman with the issue of blood who had **HEARD** of Jesus, then **SAID** (and HEARD) to herself, "...If I may touch but his clothes, I shall be whole." She pressed in to do just that and was healed of a 12-year bleeding disorder."

What is it again that we should be hearing? The Gospel of Jesus Christ; the good news of the Kingdom of God. Salvation again in the Greek is 'soteria' and indicates deliverance from anything the enemy is doing to bother us. We just have to hear the Word of the Lord concerning that particular thing and use it (wield that sword) to slice through the satan's lies. As Isaiah 54:17 promises us, *"No weapon formed against us shall prosper."* Jesus used the Written Word to ward off temptation and so must we. We must war in prayer with the Word, declaring the promises of God.

My favorite prayer tool is "Prayers that Avail Much" by Germaine Copeland.[4] In these books Copeland has formed prayers using the Word of God. She then lists the scriptures used in the prayers which gives a solid foundation of scriptures on which to stand as we fight to hold on to our faith.

While I encourage everyone to get a copy of one of the many versions of this prayer aid, until you do, Copeland also has a website where you can find many of these Word-filled prayers. https://prayers.org/search-prayer-tool/

Now is a good opportunity to spend time researching and meditating on scriptures to war with as we believe God for a manifestation of His promises in our lives. Pull out your Journey from Hope to Faith from Lesson 1 and let's find some more 'Words for our Title Deed'.

Struggling to walk according to the Word of God? Ask the Father for His help.

"…come boldly before the throne of grace to find mercy and grace to help us in our time of need."

Hebrews 4:16

"…being confident of this very thing, that He who has begun a good work in you will complete [it] until the day of Jesus Christ;"

Phil 1:6 NKJV

"[2]Grace and peace be multiplied unto you through the knowledge of God, and of Jesus our Lord, [3]According as his divine power hath given unto us all things that [pertain] unto life and godliness, through the knowledge of him that hath called us to glory and virtue: [4]Whereby are given unto us exceeding great and precious promises: that by these ye might be partakers of the divine nature, having escaped the corruption that is in the world through lust."

2Pe 1:2-4 KJV

Need God's help financially?

"And my God shall supply all your need according to His riches in glory by Christ Jesus."

Phil 4:19 NKJV

"Now he that ministereth seed to the sower both minister bread for [your] food, and multiply your seed sown, and increase the fruits of your righteousness;"

2Co 9:10

Need healing? It's promised too.

"…who Himself bore our sins in His own body on the tree, that we, having died to sins, might live for righteousness--by whose stripes you were healed."

1Pe 2:24 NKJV

"[19]Then they cry unto the LORD in their trouble, [and] he saveth them out of their distresses. [20]He sent his word, and healed them, and delivered [them] from their destructions. [21]Oh that [men] would praise the LORD [for] his goodness, and [for] his wonderful works to the children of men!"

Psa 107:19-21 KJV

Overcome with stress or grief or sorrow? Begin to thank God in the midst of the situation, acknowledging that;

"You will keep [him] in perfect peace, [Whose] mind [is] stayed [on You], Because he trusts in You."

Isa 26:3 NKJV

"Cast all your anxiety on him because he cares for you."

1Pe 5:7 NIV

Scriptures that remind us of God's omnipotence secure us in knowing that in every situation He is All Powerful and nothing is too hard for Him...nothing too hard for His Word to accomplish.

"So shall my word be that goeth forth out of my mouth: it shall not return unto me void, but it shall accomplish that which I please, and it shall prosper [in the thing] whereto I sent it."

Isa 55:11 KJV

"No weapon that is formed against thee shall prosper; and every tongue [that] shall rise against thee in judgment thou shalt condemn. This [is] the heritage of the servants of the LORD, and their righteousness [is] of me, saith the LORD."

Isa 54:17 KJV

Reflections:

1. Why is hearing the Word of God so important?

2. Can you identify an area of your life where you are not experiencing the victory you would like to see?

3. Can you see where you have not HEARD the Word of God concerning that area of your life? Identify what philosophy or 'other' words contrary to the Word of God shaped your mindset concerning that area.

4. List at least two scriptures that deal with this area?

5. Look up the word salvation in the Greek (Strongs concordance G4991) and list the many things included in this definition. (www.blueletterbible.com is a free Bible Study resource that includes Strong's references as well as Vines Expository Dictionary and many other resources on the site.)

LESSON 4
THE CONNECTION
BETWEEN
HOPE AND FAITH

*"Now **FAITH** is the **substance** of **things hoped** for, the **evidence** of **things not seen.**"*

Hebrews 11:1

The writer of Hebrews points to a definite connection between hope and faith. We, therefore, cannot possibly try to walk by faith without understanding hope and the connection between faith and hope. In lesson 1 we mentioned that Webster's 1828 dictionary defines hope as,

> *"A desire of some good, accompanied with at least a slight expectation of obtaining it, or a belief that it is obtainable."*

Hope, this desire of some good, is the starting point for faith. It is that thing which comes out of our wills that we would like to see happen at some point in the future. However, hope does *not* carry with it the same surety as faith. Fifteenth century theologian, Martin Luther, offers a summary of some of the key differences between hope and faith that includes the following three major points regarding their source, their function and their objective:

	Hope		Faith
Source / Origin	Variable/ Situational rising from the will of man		Founded on Understanding
Function	Exhorts the mind to be strong & courageous		Says, teaches, describes, directs what will be
Objective	Goodness of God		Truth

Luther's account offers that a major difference between the two is origin, or where they come from. The foundation of faith is in understanding the unchangeable truth of the Word of God, whereas hope arises out of the various situations man finds himself faced with that causes him to 'will' something different. This does not mean that hope is unnecessary. Quite the contrary, hope is necessary because it brings the issues that need change to the Word that can change them. We cannot transfer from hope to faith - wanting to see something different to actually realizing it - until we understand the truth on which to stand. The connection is therefore, understanding the truth of the Word of God concerning the 'things'.

God's enemy – satan - is continuously trying to undermine and destroy those things that either bring life to us, or bring us to our life source. John 10:10 tells us clearly that as the thief, he comes "*...but for to steal and to kill and to destroy.*" Hope is one of those things he is trying to steal from us because without it we cannot have faith, and without faith we cannot access the grace of God that is able to bring the life of God to us. Satan is especially busy in this

> **"...THEY THAT GO DOWN INTO THE PIT CANNOT HOPE FOR THY TRUTH."**
> **ISAIAH 38:18**

dispensation of time promoting a fatalistic view, one that causes a doomsday philosophy where people lose hope in the future for everything because he has made the situations of this world look so bleak. He knows that once life is over and we enter the grave, there is no hope, so he attempts to drive us there. But until we breathe our last breath - there is hope in God!

Even well-meaning Christians can be found guilty of having a fatalistic view; one that is always focused on the end-times, waiting for the tribulation - or wondering if we have already entered it. We cannot be so focused on the 'last days' that we forget that God is still here for us, that God is still good, that God still delivers, sets free, heals, restores and prospers those who put their trust in Him.

The trick of the enemy comes into play because we lose our witness to the world when we become as pessimistic as they are about the future, even in the name of supporting end-time Bible doctrine. A major part of our winning the lost is having a positive hopeful spirit that leads us to faith in the grace of God to empower us for victory even in a day where hopelessness abounds. This gives a sign to them that if you have hope then maybe all is not lost. God's people should never ever feel hopeless! It is an insult to the Almighty God to feel hopeless...to feel like whatever we are going through is beyond His reach or more powerful than He is.

Consider the times. The ultimate in hopelessness is suicide, which is on the rise in the United States. People look at temporary life situations, see no way out and make permanent decisions to end their lives. Middle schoolers and teenagers, who potentially have a full life ahead of them are tricked into thinking there is no way out. God always has a way of escape and we must never forget that. In the thick of the biggest struggles we face, God always makes a way of escape. We just have to do what David did and talk to ourselves. Remind ourselves of when God did it before and trust that He will do it again. That spark of hope is enough to build faith on.

NEVER MAKE PERMANENT DECISIONS OVER TEMPORARY SITUATIONS.

As David said in Psalm 38:15, *"In Thee O Lord do I hope. Thou wilt hear, O Lord, my God!"* God will always lend His ear to hear His children. We cannot listen to the enemy tell us that life is hopeless. David spoke to himself again in Psalm 42:5 as he wrestled with what was believed to be battle fatigue – weariness in fighting his enemies. He had to talk to himself. He told his soul – his mind, will and emotions – to *"hope thou in God who is the health of my countenance."*

He commanded his soul to praise God in the midst of what looked like a hopeless situation, knowing that praise would silence his enemy and work to restore his soul. From David we can learn, that unless we have that smidgen of hope we are doomed already. Without hope we can't see our way to even attempt to seek and understand the truth that could potentially make us free. Instead we say, "What's the use?" and give up without trying if we don't hold on to hope. Never ever give up!

Look at the Old Testament account of Naomi, who with her husband and sons had left the land of Judah during a famine to travel to the heathen country of Moab. While there, her husband and sons died and she set herself to return to Judah with only the hope of living on the kindness of her relatives. She tried to deter her daughters-in-law from going with her, telling them that there was no hope that she could produce another husband for them. Only Ruth would not budge.

Instead, God gave her and Naomi a new life that included an unexpected wealthy kinsman-redeemer who married Ruth and gave her a son (and grandson for Naomi) in the name of Ruth's late husband. She left God's promised land, returned dejected and found the God of mercy and hope still there for her. This grandson of hers, Obed, is the grandfather of King David and a part of the lineage of our Lord Jesus Christ.

Consider Job, though it appeared in the natural that he had little to look forward to after the loss of his children, his wealth, and everything but a disgruntled wife and judgmental friends. Job felt hopeless in the natural and was even encouraged by his own wife to curse God and die. He refused to do so, because God was his only hope. He knew enough about the character and goodness of God to say, ***"Though He [God] slay me, yet will I trust Him."*** (Job 13:15).

The New Testament delivers the story of the ultimate hope for believers, because it is here that we are introduced to the Savior that is a manifestation of the hope for which the world has waited since the fall of man. Jesus Christ brings to us the hope of right relationship with God the Father again and makes that possible through His shed blood on the cross of Calvary. Paul also often speaks of this blessed hope of our physical reunion with God at the second coming of Jesus Christ. This is ultimately why we never lose hope. Even when confronted with death, Paul in I Thessalonians 4:13 tells us that we should not sorrow as those who have no hope (unbelievers) because the end of this life in the natural is only the beginning of the second phase of eternal life for the believer.

So we see that all these accounts where hope is called into play arise out of various situations in life. When given a little hope, faith takes those situations, hears the Word of God concerning them and speaks new life – the life of God - into them. Hope rises out of circumstances, faith applies the Word to it and stands on the Truth it understands until it is manifested.

The second point of difference noted is in the ***function*** of hope and faith. While we just mentioned that faith stands on the truth, know also that the enemy will come for that truth, and hope rises again to fight with faith, encouraging our faith to be strong by keeping the picture of the better 'thing' before us. These two, hope and faith, continue to work hand in hand to deliver the manifestation of the promise to the believer. Faith doesn't just come and take over while hope leaves town. Hope keeps the passion of that *'thing'*, that desire before the believer, who in faith is standing on the Word of God as a title deed to say that is indeed mine! Hope says, "Don't let go faith!"

The third point of difference noted is the **object** of hope and faith. Hope is relying on the goodness of God, while faith is taking a stand on the Truth of God. While we can expect God to be good because that is His nature, what is more important for us is to rely on His Word, the Truth. This brings up the gross misunderstanding man has of the concept of sovereignty, or supreme power and authority. God is sovereign in that He is Omnipotent, ultimately in control. However, by His design, man was not created to be puppets on a string with no choices in the matters of life. God gave man something called 'free will'. He gave Adam and Even control and options and they exercised their option to believe the enemy of God instead of God. God in His sovereignty could have just snatched Adam and Eve back, but if He did so, He would have been removing man's ability to freely love or reject God Himself. Love is not love unless it is given freely. While you can force obedience and servitude through punishment, you cannot force someone to love you. Neither would God.

God is the same today. While He is the essence of good, we don't access His goodness by just hoping for it. One of the hardest scriptures in the Bible to understand conceptually is Romans 9:15 where Paul repeats something God said to Moses, *"I will have mercy on whom I will have mercy, and I will have compassion on whom I will have compassion."* When we are not coming to Him in faith, God can choose to have mercy and compassion at the pleasure of His will. However, when we come in faith according to the Truth of His Word, He moves to answer our faith because He cannot lie!

MOVING FROM HOPE TO FAITH
The connection again between hope and faith is seen in applying the Word of Truth to the situations we are hoping to see changed. This is a must if we are going to move from hope to faith. Let's look again at

our 'Hope to Faith Worksheet' from Lesson 1, which should have a little more meaning for us now. "I Hope." We start with a situation that we desire to see changed; a desire generally placed on our hearts by God Himself. It may be a generational curse, a child in trouble, a financial need or just a genuine desire for something better. The next thing we do is really seek God about His desired outcome concerning that thing. Remember as God spoke through Jeremiah in 29:11-14,

> *[11]For I know the thoughts that I think toward you, saith the LORD, thoughts of peace, and not of evil, to give you an expected end. [12]Then shall ye call upon me, and ye shall go and pray unto me, and I will hearken unto you. [13]And ye shall seek me, and find [me], when ye shall search for me with all your heart. [14]And I will be found of you, saith the LORD: and I will turn away your captivity, and I will gather you from all the nations, and from all the places whither I have driven you, saith the LORD; and I will bring you again into the place whence I caused you to be carried away captive."*

We see the next steps in this passage from Jeremiah as well. We should seek God and find God, searching for HIM with our whole hearts...not just searching for the thing. Jesus restates this principle in Matthew 6:33 in the now famous sermon on the Mount where He tells His disciples,

> **"But seek ye first the kingdom of God, and his righteousness; and all these things shall be added unto you."**

Our ultimate goal in believing God for something is to do so with a Kingdom mentality, where God's will and bringing Him glory is more important than the thing itself! The more we seek to please Him with the desires of our heart and build ourselves up in faith by hearing His Word concerning it, we will see a manifestation of those things we desire...because they are also His desires.

FROM HOPE TO FAITH FOR MY CHILD

Let me pause here and share with you some of the highlights of how my hope was turned to faith in our battle with infertility. After five years of marriage and completion of my first degree, we decided we wanted to start our family. After a year with no success, we were referred to an infertility specialist and I began a monitoring process which meant I had to take my temperature every morning to watch for signs of ovulation. The goal was to see the temperature stay up at the end of the month, which was as good as a positive pregnancy test.

Unfortunately for years I endured the torture of being reminded daily that we did not have the promise, as my temperature dropped every month. The promise, you ask, what promise? After time in prayer I believed that God would give me the desire of my heart and cause this barren woman to keep house and be the joyful mother of children according to Psalm 113:9. I sincerely asked God to remove the desire for our own biological children from us if it was not His will. We even considered adoption, but when I was ready, my husband was not. When he was ready, I had changed my mind because I had been seeking God and was convinced that we were going to have biological children.

At one point I was at a women's conference at our church and the speaker made a statement that I had heard many times before, but somehow this time it impacted me differently because I had been in the presence of God. During her message she said, "His Name is above *EVERY* name" and I heard a voice that is as close to audible as I have ever heard. The voice said, "His Name is above Infertility."

Wow! I had never considered that infertility was a name, but immediately I began to rejoice because I knew that word, spoken as a 'logos' through this woman of God had become a 'Rhema' word in my spirit and caused me to cross over from hope to faith for my child. I had been seeking God and increasing my worship relationship with Him, but with this new found revelation I worshipped Him in praise for what He had already done and began to stand on Psalm 113:9,

"He maketh the barren woman to keep house, [and to be] a joyful mother of children. Praise ye the LORD."

But more importantly, while I knew I had received the title deed for my child, ironically I knew that the relationship with God had become more important to me. I had the knowing that this child was mine, but honestly felt that even if it did not manifest, I would be fine because the joy of the Lord had secured me.

This was a seven-year battle and it was not easy at times, but as already mentioned, on those days when it seemed it would never come and my faith was in a fight, hope rose back up as a cheerleader and said, "I want this too badly for you to give up the fight." So hope joined forces with my faith and carried me across the finish line. Almost twelve years after we were married my son Brandon was born and our world rejoiced because of this new life, and God was glorified by many people who had warred with us for answering our prayer. At times during the fight it seemed like time stood still and the answer would never come, but today Brandon is 27, Jamin is 24 and Briana is 22. Today, it seems like yesterday.

So we continue to speak the Word of God over situations and as we will discuss in the upcoming lessons we put actions to our faith and learn to stand and having done all to stand, knowing that God's Word has given us the title deed for that which we are believing.

Reflections:

1. What is the connection between hope and faith?

2. Regarding the function of hope and faith, what does each of them do?

3. Explain sovereignty and free will.

4. What steps do we take to move from hope to faith?

5. What part does hope play after we have built our faith to receive the title deed for what we are believing?

Journey from Hope to Faith Worksheet
I Hope:

The Words in my Title Deed:

My confession: In the Name of Jesus, I believe that I receive…

LESSON 5
ACTIVATING FAITH

"For with the heart man believeth unto righteousness; and with the mouth confession is made unto salvation."

Rom 10:10 KJV

As discussed in Lesson 3 we set our schedules to prioritize hearing the Word of God. Now that we are building it, what actions do we take to put our faith to work for us? Romans 10:10 holds the key to understanding how we begin to do this. Here Paul informs us that in our hearts we **believe** to get back into a place of right relationship with God. But we really don't begin to see faith at work until we carry out the second phrase of this verse: **confess with our mouths unto salvation**. In other words, we have to speak from our position of faith to usher in the salvation that we are believing for. Remember that salvation is deliverance from the molestation or 'bothering' of our enemy. We can silence the enemy of our souls by speaking the Word of God against him. Our 'heart change' causes the right relationship with God, but the words we speak seal the deal and bring God's deliverance into manifestation in our lives.

Notice here that the King James version uses the word 'confession' to describe *the speaking part of our salvation experience*. Let's take a minute to define and talk about the four different types of confession that are mentioned in scripture, and determine which one applies to our lesson today.

1. The Jewish Confession of sin under the Old Covenant
2. The Sinner's Confession under the New Covenant
3. The Believer's Confession of his sins
4. The Believer's Confession of Faith

1. The Jewish Confession of sin under the Old Covenant

The **Jewish confession of sin** is the type of confession that John led people into as he baptized them 'unto repentance' in the Jordan at the beginning of the New Testament (cf. Mark 1:4,5). This was an awakening of their responsibilities to confess or speak their sins, acknowledging their shortcomings under the Old Covenant. But John could only lead them to the place of remembering that they were nothing without God and needed to repent and humble themselves before Him to prepare for what God was getting ready to do through 'He that cometh after...'" Paul confirms this in Acts 13.

> *"Before he came, John the Baptist preached that all the people of Israel needed to repent of their sins and turn to God and be baptized."*
>
> *Acts 13:24 (NLT)*

2. The Sinner's Confession under the New Covenant

This practice was fulfilled thanks to the death, burial and resurrection of Jesus Christ as we see the second type of confession come into play. Jesus Himself, in John 16:7-11 tells us that the Holy Spirit, the Godhead agent of the New Testament church, is said to convict the world of 'sin' (a singular word) because the world didn't believe on Jesus. Our **confession in receiving salvation** is speaking with our mouths that Jesus Christ is Lord and that God has raised Him from the dead. After the death, burial and resurrection of Christ, unbelief is the only sin God holds against us. Once we confess our faith in Jesus Christ we are in right relationship with God again.

But God knows our soul is still wrestling to be made into the image of Christ and we are likely to commit sin in this process.

3. The Believer's Confession of his sins

If and when we sin after becoming believers, He has made provision for us to be restored immediately, by the third type of confession – **believers confessing our sins to Him** when we mess up, knowing that

> *"If we confess our sins, he is faithful and just to forgive us [our] sins, and to cleanse us from all unrighteousness."*
>
> *I John 1:9*

Pay attention again to the context of this passage in I John 1. John is talking to believers who sin, not sinners who have never received Christ. We maintain right relationship with God with our obedience. Because He is committed to that relationship He has made a way for us to maintain it even when we miss the mark in the process of working out our soul salvation. We can come to Him, confess our sins and in faith expect that He not only forgives us, but cleanses us from unrighteousness and gives us grace to overcome.

4. The Believer's Confession of Faith

The final mention of confession in scripture refers to the believers' **confession of faith**. This is the key way that we activate our faith for the promises of God. After salvation, our confession of faith is critical because it covers our setting out on a course of yielding to Him as Lord. If the enemy could not keep us from receiving Christ as Savior, then he spends the rest of our lives trying to silence us from our confession of faith because this is **the act of the believer declaring the provisions of His new covenant with God**.

Jesus gave us these instructions in Mark 11:22-24 as he left us *His* Word concerning the power of what we say:

> *²²And Jesus answering saith unto them, Have faith in God. ²³For verily I say unto you, That whosoever shall <u>say</u> unto this mountain, Be thou removed, and be thou cast into the sea; and shall not doubt in his heart, but shall believe that those things which he <u>saith</u> shall come to pass; he <u>shall have whatsoever he saith</u>. ²⁴Therefore I say unto you, What things soever ye desire, when ye pray, believe that ye receive [them], and ye shall have [them].*

Jesus' instruction is that we speak to the situation (mountain), and then He declares that if we believe what we say as we pray we will have whatever we say. He also demonstrated the power of speaking the Word as He was tempted of the devil in the wilderness. Each time the enemy approached him, Jesus said, "It is written." He didn't just 'think it' or 'mediate on it' in His heart, He spoke the written Word of God and then told the devil to get away from him. Guess what the devil did? He got away from him! It works the same for us. When we walk in the principles of the Word as we are led by His Spirit and speak it regularly, the devil will also not be able to stand before us.

71

What Are *You* Saying?

In Mark 11, Jesus Himself teaches us the importance of what we say, highlighting two key points:

1. *Whatever we say*
2. *not doubting in our hearts, but believing*

In the instruction Jesus gives here on receiving in faith, we see Him making the connection between what is in our hearts and what comes out of our mouths. He says that if we believe when we pray, not doubting in our hearts, then we will have what we say. In Matthew 12:35 we see why this is true: The words of our mouth are actually a reflection of what is in our hearts. This passage in Matthew 12:33-37, highlights that there has to be consistency in our words and our lifestyle. What we say and how we conduct our daily lives is what really speaks concerning what we believe.

> [34]*...For out of the abundance of the heart the mouth speaks.* [35]*"A good man out of the good treasure of his heart brings forth good things, and an evil man out of the evil treasure brings forth evil things.* [36]*"But I say to you that for every idle word men may speak, they will give account of it in the day of judgment.* [37]*"For by your words you will be justified, and by your words you will be condemned."*
>
> Matt. 12:33-37 NKJV

When we claim that we believe when we pray, then walk away from prayer saying the opposite of what we are praying for, this hinders us from receiving from God. Proof that we believe is seen in what we say and do after we get up off our knees and walk out of our prayer closets. Matthew tells us in this passage in the 12th chapter that our words will reveal what we truly believe in our hearts, and as Jesus said, we must believe that we receive what we say, when we pray.

This process of walking out our faith with our words and actions does not generally happen overnight. Initially, we have to learn NOT to speak the reality of the facts, but instead the results that we want to see according to the Word of God. Some people may try to call us liars and say that we are in denial when we speak the Word. On the contrary, we are not denying the natural existence of the facts, we are just denying their right to lord over us. We are citizens of another kingdom now – the Kingdom of God – and His words 'lord' or prevail over those facts and we receive by faith the results of God. The more we speak it, the more we are cooperating with the Spirit in bringing a manifestation of it into our lives.

Years ago I heard my pastor, Timothy R. Stokes I make the statement that "the person God promises the blessing to is usually not the one who receives it." He said this because we go through a transformational process in receiving it. When we learn to speak the Word of God concerning the things we are believing Him for, we find ourselves changing into that person who is called to receive the blessing and transported to the place where the blessing may have been waiting for us all along.

Don't Forget: Faith works through Grace
As important as faith is in receiving the things we hope for from God I want to make sure we are balanced in our understanding of why it works. Lesson 2 clearly taught us that the primary purpose of our faith is to access the grace of God. It is God's grace – *His unmerited favor* – that provides the 'things' for which we are believing. So in the process of speaking the Word in faith we should never walk away in arrogance thinking that we have some super level of faith that gets us anything we want from God. The truth is, our faith just taps into His grace, His favor, which according to James 4:6 is only available to the humble.

> *"But He gives more grace. Therefore, He says: "God resists the proud, but gives grace to the humble."*
> *James 4:6 NKJV*

We must be Led by the Spirit to Activate our Faith
Luke's account of the temptation of Jesus says in chapter 4 verse 1 that Jesus was led into the wilderness *by the Spirit* of God to be tempted of the devil. After defeating him with the Word of the Lord, verse 14 tells us that Jesus then went forth in the power of the Spirit. We cannot forget the role of Holy Spirit in actually receiving that for which we are believing God.

Consider the creation story. Holy Spirit hovered over the chaos that was to be changed, waiting for the Word to be spoken. Holy Spirit is a critical part of bringing the Word to pass. Even involving Jesus becoming the Word of God made flesh to dwell among us, Mary conceived of the Holy Spirit. Throughout the New Testament we find account after account of Holy Spirit moving to bring to pass the Word of the Lord.

This is especially important to understand as we move to act on the Word of the Lord as an expression of our faith. We must wait to be led by Holy Spirit to do what He leads us to, otherwise we are moving presumptuously, acting out of our own will to make something happen, and we are subject to get fleshly results instead of the will of the Father.

Combine this with the words of James, who said the following:

> *22But be ye <u>doers of the word</u>, and not hearers only, deceiving your own selves. 23For if any be a hearer of the word, and <u>not a doer</u>, he is <u>like unto a man beholding his natural face in a glass:</u> 24For he beholdeth himself, and goeth his way, and straightway forgetteth what manner of man he was. 25But <u>whoso</u> looketh into the perfect law of liberty, and <u>continueth</u> [therein], he being not a forgetful hearer, but a <u>doer of the work,</u> this man shall be blessed in his deed. 26If any man among you seem to be religious, and <u>bridleth not his tongue,</u> but deceiveth his own heart, this man's <u>religion [is] vain.</u> James 1:22-26*

James, is the biological 'little brother' of Jesus and watched him grow up. I'm sure after Jesus' death on the cross James began to re-live childhood moments where he saw Jesus growing "…in wisdom, and stature and in favor with God and man." (Luke 2:52 NIV). James is highlighting, in his short, five-chapter epistle - not that our words aren't important - but that actions speak louder than just words. Jesus said whoever says without doubting in his heart would see the mountain move. What we believe in our hearts will show up in our actions as they line up with the words that we speak. Faith in the Word is reflected in doing the Word as we are led by Holy Spirit to specifically act on that Word!

People get frustrated waiting on a manifestation of what they have 'faith' for when they are speaking one thing and doing the opposite, as if their words alone are a magical incantation that will change the situation. While we begin to confess the word as we build our faith, we also follow Holy Spirit's lead as we begin to change our 'conversation' or lifestyle to match the words we speak. That is the confession that brings a manifestation of the power of God into our lives.

Our lifestyles should glorify God, and Holy Spirit is there to speak to us with instructions and directions on how to walk in the newness of life that is laid out in the Word of God. But we must listen to His Voice when He speaks.

- Why confess healing but refuse to change our diet and exercise habits?
- Why confess financial increase but refuse to become good stewards of the resources God has already given us?
- Why believe God for a new job if we are not faithfully working the one we have now?

In actuality, if we listen for His direction, Holy Spirit will lead us to walk according to the principles of the Word of God so that we do not have to be so focused on using our faith for 'things' and can instead be focused on what we started this series talking about…faith to fulfill our calling and in the process winning souls and making disciples.

These are the conflicts that cause people to question God's goodness, His fairness and His grace, when it is usually our actions, or lack of following Holy Spirit, that hinder the move of God. This also damages our good witness to the world; when they hear us 'confessing' the Word but not receiving. They question whether or not our God hears us when we pray because they see no results. Let's make our lives line up with the Word and be led by Holy Spirit so that we can watch as God is glorified when we receive what we say. Jesus Himself said,

> *"And whatsoever ye shall ask in my name, that will I do, that the Father may be glorified in the Son."*
> *John 14:13*

James also says in the second chapter of his epistle that faith without works is dead. Though he was primarily talking here about demonstrating a lifestyle of faith as evidenced by doing the works of caring for the poor, the principle still holds for faith for other things in our lives as well.

> *⁴What [doth it] profit, my brethren, though a man say he hath faith, and have not works? can faith save him?...¹⁷Even so faith, if it hath not works, is dead, being alone.*
> *James 2:4, 17*

Watch out for the Fear Factor

While every believer is encouraged to walk in faith, doing deeds that show what is truly in our hearts, recognize also that some will out of fear walk in a way that denies the reality of negative situations in their lives. For example, faith does not make us afraid to go to the doctor and listen to what he or she has to say regarding a medical condition. Faith instead will take a 'bad report' and put the Word on it, waiting for the leading of Holy Spirit concerning how to walk in faith concerning the healing. I know some who out of fear have denied that they have cancer, feeling like they are not in faith if they take chemotherapy or other treatments to fight the disease. Jesus Himself said,

> *And Jesus answering said unto them, They that are whole need not a physician; but they that are sick.*
> *Luke 5:31*

There are some who will be led to take the medical route for their healing and others who will be specifically led to believe God without the intervention of medical science. If you are faced with that dilemma, determine your level of faith and believe God for what you can believe God for: If your faith is where you can believe that God will work through the medical doctors to affect your healing, then be healed in Jesus' name!

Revisiting the Infertility Case
In my case we worked with medical professionals but they didn't offer much hope. After my crossover from hope to faith the battle only intensified but as I stated earlier hope rose up to encourage my faith. I was hearing from friends who were dreaming I was pregnant and praying and receiving confirmation in their prayer time that this baby was on the way. But in the natural, nothing seemed to be going right. I decided to suspend my visits to the specialist because I needed a mental break. I also did not want to see another basal temperature thermometer!

Then in 1989 I went to church with my brother-in-law Kenny and his family in Louisiana. The next day he called me to tell me one of the ladies at their church wanted to talk to me. I immediately knew it was about my baby. I called and Margie related the following experience to me.

She was on the prayer team at the church, but obviously had a faithful prayer life outside the church. She said she had been in prayer one day and God began to show her this lady who was crying and wouldn't stop. After a while (and getting tired of seeing this lady crying) she asked God why was she crying. The Lord told her that this lady wanted a baby but couldn't have one. Margie began to pray for this lady she saw in her prayer time and then related the incident to the prayer team at her church. They had Margie stand in the middle of a circle 'in proxy' for the lady and began to lay hands on her and prayer that God would open her womb. She then told me that as she was walking out of the door of the church that night before, she turned and saw me out of the corner of her eye. When she laid her eyes on me she said the Holy Spirit spoke to her and said, "That's the woman you have been praying for!"

Needless to say I was overwhelmed at the love of God: that He would have a group of women 1,100 miles away from me, in my husband's hometown praying for me! My family there was equally excited and the people in Michigan who had been standing in faith with me were thrilled. This stirred my faith all over again. But we were not done yet.

Pray, Believe, Speak and Be Led!

So activating our faith is not just magically reciting a few scriptures like a witch's incantation. We must speak what we believe in our hearts, and be led by the Spirit of God to walk in a way that shows what we believe in our hearts. Wherever our faith is, we need to walk tall in it and not be ashamed that it is not at the same level as someone else. We must mind our own garden and grow our own mustard seed of faith! Believe according to where you are.

What does the new believer confess and begin to do? Whatever the scripture says we are in Christ. Refer to the attachment in Lesson 3 on the scriptures for our promises.

Scripture exercise

We see example after example in scripture to support speaking the word, then acting in a way that demonstrates that you believe. As you go through the following scriptures, highlight or underline the actions taken by the person making the request.

> *47 When this man heard that Jesus had arrived in Galilee from Judea, he went to him and begged him to come and heal his son, who was close to death...49 The royal official said, "Sir, come down before my child dies." 50 "Go," Jesus replied, "your son will live." The man took Jesus at his word and departed. 51 While he was still on the way, his servants met him with the news that his boy was living.*
> *John 4:47-51 (NIV)*

> *4 When he had finished speaking, he said to Simon, "Put out into deep water, and let down the nets for a catch." 5 Simon answered, "Master, we've worked hard all night and haven't caught anything. But because you say so, I will let down the nets." 6 When*

they had done so, they caught such a large number of fish that their nets began to break.

Luke 5:4-6 (NIV)

[6] "Lord," he said, "my servant lies at home paralyzed, suffering terribly." [7] Jesus said to him, "Shall I come and heal him?" [8] The centurion replied, "Lord, I do not deserve to have you come under my roof. But just say the word, and my servant will be healed... [13] Then Jesus said to the centurion, "Go! Let it be done just as you believed it would." And his servant was healed at that moment.

Matthew 8:6-8, 13 (NIV)

[28] "Lord, if it's you," Peter replied, "tell me to come to you on the water." [29] "Come," he said. Then Peter got
down out of the boat, walked on the water and came toward Jesus.
Matthew 14:28-29 (NIV)
"Go," he told him, "wash in the Pool of Siloam" (this word means "Sent"). So the man went and washed, and came home seeing.
John 9:7 (NIV)

[20] And, behold, a woman, which was diseased with an issue of blood twelve years, came behind [him], and touched the hem of his garment: [21] For she said within herself, If I may but touch his garment, I shall be whole. [22] But Jesus turned him about, and when he saw her, he said, Daughter, be of good comfort; thy faith hath made thee whole. And the woman was made whole from that hour.

Matthew 9:20-22 (KJV)

Reflections

1. What 2 things does Romans 10:10 tell us we must do to receive salvation?

2. Describe confession?

3. How do we silence the enemy of our soul?

4. What is the only thing the sinner needs to confess under the New Covenant? Give scripture support.

5. What should we do if we sin after receiving Christ as Savior? What should we expect God to do in return? Give scripture support.

6. What key way do we activate our faith after salvation? Give scripture support.

7. What is the role of Holy Spirit in activating faith?

8. Why is the confession of our faith so important to our walk in Christ?

9. What does Jesus' little brother James say must be done to make faith effective?

10. What specifically should believers continually confess?

Let's spend some time now looking at the Word of God concerning different areas of our lives and learn to write out prayers based upon the Word of God. Let's retrain ourselves to speak His Word instead of the facts that describe defeat and a life that is less than what God desires for us.

If you don't already own the book, Prayers that Avail Much by Germaine Copeland, I encourage you to purchase one of its many versions. In the meantime, you can go the website https://prayers.org/search-prayer-tool/ and access many of them by typing in the area of concern. Focus on just one area of your life and look up and write out the scriptures listed at the end of the prayer for that issue. You may also want to do a Bible word search for other scripture promises related to that matter. Write out a prayer, based on the Word of God that speaks in faith what you believe God has done for you in this area of your life.

I'M PRAYING THE WORD

Prayer focus:

Write out your scripture support: The known will of God concerning this matter.

LESSON 6
THE FIGHT OF FAITH

"Fight the good fight of faith, lay hold on eternal life, whereunto thou art also called, and hast professed a good profession before many witnesses."

I Timothy 6:12

Paul tells Timothy, his spiritual son, that faith does not always bring instant results. Instead, we have to be prepared to fight what he calls a ***good fight of faith***. His main focus here is on fighting to persevere when being persecuted, but the principle holds true for anything for which we are believing God.

What does the fight look like? Paul tells the Corinthian church that it is *NOT* a battle fought in our flesh.

³For though we walk in the flesh, we do not war after the flesh: ⁴ (For the weapons of our warfare [are] not carnal, but mighty through God to the pulling down of strong holds;)

II Corinthians 10:3-4

The weapons used in our fight of faith are not carnal or manmade, but weapons in the spirit that are mighty THROUGH GOD for the purpose of pulling down strongholds. Notice that Paul said that our weapons are mighty *through God*...not our own strength, power, or wisdom, but weapons that rely on God's mighty power. Our natural, carnal strength and wisdom are no match for an enemy who has been at this game for thousands of years. God's power is the only power that can defeat him and win our battles. So we must first of all quit trying to fight with natural human resources that have not been sanctioned nor commissioned by the Spirit of God.

Remember the story of David and Goliath? David had several opportunities to blow it by resorting to natural tools to try to defeat this giant. First of all, scary King Saul offered his big armor to David. Mind you, Saul was too scared to fight him, but he sent this teenage volunteer to do his job. David refused, saying he wasn't familiar with Saul's weapons, he had not 'proven' them in battle. David needed to fight with what he was used to in killing the lion and the bear. Then again, Goliath tried to fight David on his ground, telling him to come to him. David knew better than to fight the enemy on his terms, on his ground. Instead, he told Goliath, you come to me. David stood His ground and because he stayed where he needed to be he was able to slay Goliath with a slingshot and five smooth stones. God uses the foolish things of this world to confound the wise. Who would have thought that this teenager could beat the giant, but especially with a slingshot.

Then Paul goes on to talk about the purpose of the weapons; what we are to use them for in this fight of faith. He said they are designed to pull down strongholds, so we must understand what strongholds are to give us further insight into what the good fight of faith is like.

Strongholds, according to Strong's Biblical concordance are fortified walls that safely hold [and protect] something; in this case thoughts that are contrary to the Word of God. Vine's Expository Dictionary calls a stronghold a 'fortress' designed in this context to defend our carnal human thoughts against the light of God's Word. So our fight of faith is about tearing down those thoughts and ideologies; those worldviews that are not based upon the Word of God - and there are many of them these days! As we dismantle them, we build new strongholds with the Word of God, allowing Him to be our stronghold against the enemy that would try to discourage our faith.

> *"...THE LORD IS THE STRONGHOLD OF MY LIFE~ OF WHOM SHALL I BE AFRAID?" PSALM 27:1B*

Remember that our fight is a fight to hold on to our faith - our trust that God's Word is truth and that it will prevail for us! Too often in the heat of the battle, we focus on the natural circumstances and want to 'do something' about them with the natural means to which we have become accustomed. And this is where we find the real enemy that we are fighting, those impatient thoughts that try to tell us to get the answer some other way besides waiting on God to show up. When the answer is delayed the enemy will bring up options to the Word, and even try to make them seem like logical, godly ways to get the promise, reminding us of the myth that "God helps those who help themselves." But most of us know in our 'knower' when we are heading down a path that God has not authorized…You know that "Something" (Holy Spirit's nickname) that causes a little unrest when we first turn in that unauthorized direction? We must pay attention to Him to save ourselves a lot of time and heartache.

In order to effectively battle strongholds, Romans 12:2 gives us instruction to have our minds renewed with the Word of God. We must drown out carnal, worldly thoughts by focusing continuously on the Word. This is not a once or twice a week visit to our churches, but daily studying, daily worshipping, daily praying and creating an environment around us that invites the Spirit of God to come in and change what Joyce Meyer calls our 'stinking thinking.' When we do this regularly, we will learn how to be led by the Spirit of God and end up in that place where our answer is. This way we will get there much sooner than if we try to take the detours and shortcuts the enemy presents to us because with God, who we are becoming in the process is more important than the 'thing' waiting for us. Let's look at some examples of this.

Let's say you are believing for a mate? The world is increasingly denouncing celibacy and marriage. Stinking thinking used to say that you need to "see if this is going to work out before you get the papers", (but even this has escalated to 'it's just a piece of paper'). While the 'waiting game' is a challenge and tests your self-confidence and self-esteem, we must still stand in faith that if we follow God's Word he will grant us the desire of our hearts. We must still hold on to the 'old-fashioned' Bible doctrine given in I Cor. 6:13 that "…the body is not for fornication, but for the Lord…" Paul then urges the single believers in verse 18 to "flee fornication." It may not be popular, but it's still God's way and if we want to see His results and end up with a mate that will be a "blessing of the Lord" that enriches our lives and "addeth no sorrow with it", then we have to do it His way. Marriage can be a challenge with two godly people working to become one, so we need to avoid the extra struggle of being unequally yoked together with someone whose only match to us is body parts.

There are obviously Biblical examples of believers' being impatient and trying to manufacture God's blessings in their lives as well. Remember the father of our faith, Abraham? Remember his relationship with Hagar that produced a son Ishmael, whose descendants to this day are still fighting the descendants of Isaac, the son God promised he would have with his wife. Ishmael is the father of the Arab nations and Isaac is the father of Israel. God's way is the best way.

Paul seems to do the most talking in the New Testament about standing in faith. In Ephesians 6 he gives us detailed instructions on being armed for the battle, again emphasizing that our strongest weapon is the Word of God.

> [10]*Finally, my brethren, be strong in the Lord, and in the power of his might.*
> [11]*Put on the whole armour of God, that ye may be able to stand against the wiles of the devil.*
> [12]*For we wrestle not against flesh and blood, but against principalities, against powers, against the rulers of the darkness of this world, against spiritual wickedness in high [places].*
> [13]*Wherefore take unto you the whole armour of God, that ye may be able to withstand in the evil day, and having done all, to stand.*
> [14]*Stand therefore, having your loins girt about with truth, and having on the breastplate of righteousness;*
> [15]*And your feet shod with the preparation of the gospel of peace;*
> [16]*Above all, taking the shield of faith, wherewith ye shall be able to quench all the fiery darts of the wicked.*
> [17]*And take the helmet of salvation, and the sword of the Spirit, which is the word of God:*
> [18]*Praying always with all prayer and supplication in the Spirit, and watching thereunto with all perseverance and supplication for all saints;*
> *Ephesians 6:10-18*

He starts off again by saying that we are to be strong in the Lord and in the power of **His** might, reminding us that we are not fighting against flesh and blood, but against unseen forces. Paul then tells us to put on the armor of God in order to fight against the 'wiles' of the devil. Wiles is from the Greek '***methodeia***'[1] which means crafty, cunning, deceitful plans that someone lays in wait to spring upon you. Our enemy is crafty and cunning and out to deceive us.

The two greatest examples of his deceitful ways are found in the garden and in the wilderness. In Genesis 3:1 we find him questioning Eve about the integrity of God's Word. He asked her, 'Did God really say…?" The temptation was not as much about the actual tree of the knowledge of good and evil as it was a challenge of her belief in God's Word. Okay Eve, who will you trust?

In Jesus' wilderness temptation, the enemy again directly challenged God's Word in two of the three temptations to Christ, saying to Him, "If you are the Son of God." God had just declared in the presence of John and others at the Jordan river where Jesus was baptized, that "this is my beloved Son." In the final temptation he attempts to convince Jesus that he can give Him –the Son of God - everything that Adam had turned over to him if Jesus would just "bow down and worship him." Bowing down to worship or obey satan would have just put satan in the position of lord over His life, and Jesus was way too wise to fall for that trick like Adam and Eve did. We have to learn from our Lord's example. Giving in to the enemy's plan would mean that he is our lord, calling the shots in our lives. Instead we must do to him what Jesus did; put a little Word on him. Tell the enemy what is written concerning you and then command him to get out of your face!

Now let's take a detailed look at the armor we wage war with. First there is the **girdle of truth**. Okay ladies, we especially know first-hand what a girdle is. That piece of underwear is tight and uncomfortable at times, but it brings all the looseness together so that we can stand 'firm' and in confidence when we walk. We are not worried about 'stuff' hanging out, because our girdle is holding it together. That's what the truth does for us. It binds us, and in what sounds like a contradiction, makes us free to walk in liberty and with confidence.

Notice that it is our loins that are girt about with truth. Our loins, according to the Biblical definition are the place where our procreative, generative powers reside. In other words, those places from which we create life need to be pulled together and covered with the truth of God's Word. God doesn't want us producing or giving birth to anything that is not conceived in His truth.

The **breastplate of righteousness** is next. Our breastplate covers our hearts. Ours should be covered with the realization of who we are, those who are in right relationship with God. Remember too that out of the abundance of the heart the mouth speaks, so everything we say should be from our rightful position as sons and daughters of the Most High God. Jesus made this position possible for us and we need to honor Him by walking confidently in it; not as shy, timid individuals who don't think we deserve it, but as those who have been given the spirit of power, and of love, and of a sound mind.

Our **feet should be covered with peace**. Everywhere we go, we should be ambassadors of Shalom, peace, nothing missing, nothing broken. We should not be caught up in drama and selfishness, but as commanded in Colossians 3:15 letting peace be our umpire – the controlling factor in our hearts. We must prepare to walk like this: It does not naturally happen. We meditate on the Word of God and settle in our hearts and minds who we are in Christ. Then His peace that passes all understanding will guard our hearts and minds. When we walk like we believe this then we represent the 'good news' of peace; people notice that we are not anxious about life situations like others around us and they want to hear the good news of how we can live with such security. Then we have an open door to share our faith.

The **shield of faith** is a second covering to protect us from the fiery darts – lies – that the enemy fires our way. We must be built up in our most holy faith in order to have the protection of this shield. This means constantly hearing the Word of God and praying in the Spirit regularly. Notice that Paul says that our faith can protect us against ALL the fiery darts of the enemy. There is not one weapon that the enemy can use against us that faith will not protect us from! He is reminding us of what the prophet Isaiah said,

*No weapon that is formed against thee shall prosper;
and every tongue [that] shall rise against thee in
judgment thou shalt condemn. This [is] the heritage
of the servants of the LORD, and their righteousness
[is] of me, saith the LORD.*

Isa 54:17

Next he mentions the **helmet of salvation**. First and foremost, we are to understand in our minds that salvation, our *'soteria'*, covers our heads. Our thinking should be with the thoughts of our Savior, our Redeemer. And according to the Apostle Paul, we must fight to take down the thoughts that are contrary to the words of our God.

*Casting down imaginations, and every high thing
that exalteth itself against the knowledge of God, and
bringing into captivity every thought to the
obedience of Christ;*

II Cor. 10:5

Finally, Paul tells us to take up the **Sword of the Spirit**, which is the Word of God. This is the only offensive weapon mentioned in this passage. Paul point-blankly declares that this weapon is the Word of God! But, we must know the Word to fight with the Word. We cannot wield a sword we don't have, but if we have it then we can use it to pierce the darkness. We can use it to silence our enemy. Remember what Jesus did in the wilderness? He wielded that sword, telling the enemy, "It is written," then the enemy left him.

We have to fight God's way in order to stand and having done all, to stand. It is the enemy's desire to pull us off God's turf into a fight on his playground using his rules. Fighting the devil's way will exhaust our physical, carnal nature as we try to defend a spiritual opponent with natural carnal tools. It has never worked, and it won't ever work!

Finally she conceives!
After returning home from the overwhelming experience in Louisiana where I found that God had a prayer team who didn't even know me, praying for me, I was expecting to be pregnant the next month. But 10 months later, nothing! Instead I went back to my specialist to

actually find some devastating news. A medical test revealed pre-cancerous cells and I was told that I needed to be in the hospital three days later. My doctor informed me that regardless to the outcome of the procedure I would be put on cancer-fighting medication and not even be able to try to conceive for at least three months…and that was the best possible scenario offered.

I went home and became intimately acquainted with the term 'righteous indignation.' I got on my face in prayer before God and cried out for healing in my body. I told God that I didn't want to wait even three more months before I could try and then began to bind the spirit of infertility. I stayed in prayer until I felt a release in my spirit that things were settled. This was height of my fight. I refused to waive a white flag but instead declared war on the enemy and took back my health.

To make a long story short, I had the procedure but this time the test results were negative. Remember that my specialist said I still needed to go on medication for three months? After the procedure he didn't even mention it and instead of being on medication for three months, at the end of that time I was one month pregnant! Glory to God!

God's timing was different than what I would have chosen, but I do believe my children were born according to their purpose. In the process I received a deeper relationship with Him, with three beautiful children as a bonus.

Since that time I have been anointed to pray for other women who were struggling with infertility and watched them conceive after I prayed for them. Our fight for faith is never just about us. We win so that we can lead others to victory! So don't give up, someone else's victory is tied to yours.

As I was preparing this lesson I received the following message from my niece J'andria in Louisiana. This says it all.

> *"The fight is a fixed fight. God just wants to see if you're gonna fight to the end!"*

Reflections

1. What is the biggest faith fight you are in right now?

2. What carnal tools are you being tempted to fight with?

3. What options are the enemy giving you to get an answer quicker than waiting on God? Consider the possible destructive end of those options, as John 10:10 warns us that the enemy's ways lead to destruction.

4. What "it is written" are you prepared to fight with?

5. What fights have you won in the past? Encourage yourself in the Lord by remembering that if He did it before, He can do it again.

LESSON 7
SHARING YOUR FAITH

Sharing our faith is so much more than just telling people about the cross. It is living a life that demonstrates the effectiveness of Jesus' sacrifice. It is living a life that offers hope to others because of the hope they see active in our lives.

> "...AND I PRAY THAT THE SHARING OF YOUR FAITH MAY BECOME EFFECTIVE FOR THE FULL KNOWLEDGE OF EVERY GOOD THING THAT IS IN US FOR THE SAKE OF CHRIST."
> PHILEMON 1:6

Sharing our faith also means getting involved in people's lives; violating the rule of 'mind your own business.' Sharing our faith often means asking questions and pushing past the 'No' signs that people put up to check our real interest level: *Do you care enough to persist for me?'* As the saying goes, people don't care how much you know, until they know how much you care.

Paul commended Philemon's love and faith in the first part of his letter to this man of God. He prayed that the sharing of his faith would become effective for the full knowledge of every good thing that is in us for the sake of Christ. So we don't hold back from sharing good, in word or deed when we have the opportunity to do so for Christ's sake.

Consider the friends of the paralytic in Mark 2.

> *"³Then they came to Him, bringing a paralytic who was carried by four [men]. ⁴And when they could not come near Him because of the crowd, they uncovered the roof where He was. So when they had broken through, they let down the bed on which the paralytic was lying. ⁵When Jesus saw their faith, He said to the paralytic, "Son, your sins are forgiven you."*
> *Mark 2:3-5*

In this account of the paralytic being healed, it is because four friends carried him to see Jesus. Four friends got together and gave of themselves to help someone who could not help himself. As a result of these friends sharing their faith, the man was healed. Notice the passage indicates that Jesus saw 'their' faith. Who are we having faith for? Who is God going to save, heal and restore because 'we' have faith for them? Who are we sharing our faith with?

Look at all the details of what his friends did for him. They carried him when he could not bring himself to Jesus. They were not discouraged by the challenges of getting him there. They were persistent. They had the nerve to damage someone else's property so that their friend could be healed...and more importantly they had to have believed that he would be healed or they definitely would not have gone through all that trouble to get him to Jesus.

When they had broken a hole in the roof of a stranger's house, they began to lower their friend down into the presence of the Lord Jesus. Those are good friends! Mark then says that Jesus 'saw' their faith, then He spoke words to their friend that brought deliverance to him.

Consider another case in Acts 8:26-31, 35, 37 NKJV.

> *[26] Now an angel of the Lord spoke to Philip, saying, "Arise and go..." [27] So he arose and went. And behold, a man of Ethiopia, a eunuch of great authority under Candace the queen of the Ethiopians, who had charge of all her treasury, and had come to Jerusalem to worship, [28] was returning. And sitting in his chariot, he was reading Isaiah the prophet. [29] Then the Spirit said to Philip, "Go near and overtake this chariot." [30] So Philip ran to him, and heard him reading the prophet Isaiah, and said, "Do you understand what you are reading?" [31] And he said, "How can I, unless someone guides me?" And he asked Philip to come up and sit with him.*
>
> *[35] Then Philip opened his mouth, and...preached Jesus to him...[37] And he answered and said, "I believe that Jesus Christ is the Son of God."*

In this account Philip was instructed and led by the Holy Spirit to go to a man who turned out to be an Ethiopian eunuch who was a servant of Queen Candace. Philip approached his limo...I mean his chariot...and asked him if he understood what he was reading. Philip could've been intimidated by who this Ethiopian was for several reasons, but instead he followed the prompting of the Holy Spirit and shared his faith with him resulting in this man's salvation and baptism.

FOR GOD HAS NOT GIVEN US A SPIRIT OF FEAR, BUT OF POWER AND OF LOVE AND OF A SOUND MIND.
II TIM. 1:7 NKJV

How many times have we been timid about approaching certain people who might be in different dimensions of life than we are? They might be wealthy or poor; educated or uneducated; loud or timidly quiet; different race or ethnic group or religion; younger or older, and the enemy might tempt us to shrink back in fear about approaching them because they are different.

In God's eyes, there are two types of people; those who are in His Kingdom, and those who are not. Plain and simple. Cut and dry. They are either on their way to heaven or on their way to hell. They are either living in victory or living in defeat. We cannot look at other irrelevant differences and be scared to share our faith with them. There are wealthy, healthy, educated, outspoken of all races who need Christ. There are also poor, sick, uneducated and timid people of all races who need Christ. We must follow Holy Spirit's lead and share Jesus.

In following Holy Spirit's lead, we must also remember what Paul says in his first letter to the Corinthians.

> *⁵Who then is Paul, and who [is] Apollos, but ministers through whom you believed, as the Lord gave to each one? ⁶I planted, Apollos watered, but God gave the increase. ⁷So then neither he who plants is anything, nor he who waters, but God who gives the increase. ⁸Now he who plants and he who waters are one, and each one will receive his own reward according to his own labor.*
>
> *I Cor. 3:5-8 NKJV*

When we hear mandates from our churches that urge us to win the lost, we cannot simply pounce upon people and just invite them to church without Holy Spirit guidance. We listen for His wisdom and approach as He directs. He may be leading some of us to plant in someone's life for the first time, water where someone else has planted, or possibly be the one privileged to lead that person to Christ. None of the three (or more) in that process is better than the other, nor should the one who planted or watered feel inept because he didn't hear the salvation decision first hand. Each had a part to play and the glory belongs to God because that person is now in the Kingdom of God.

I will never forget how we planted and watered in my sister's life for years, holding on in faith that she would be saved. After about 20 years of believing God for the victory in her life another believer outside the family called and asked her if she wanted to receive Jesus as her Savior and she responded "Yes." Then she asked her do you want to do it now, and she said "Yes." She began from that point on living like II Cor. 5:7 declares, as a new creature in Christ, with old things passed away and all things made new. And we can all rejoice now because she is in the Kingdom of God, and we all had a part to play in the victory.

Remember too that sharing our faith is sharing our testimony of what God has done for us. It is sharing by modeling a new faith-filled victorious life. What has the Lord done for you? Don't be ashamed to tell it. Don't act like it's nothing, or just good luck. Somebody needs to hear of His goodness, and He is counting on us to tell it. Share your faith!

We should also commit to learning the basics of witnessing, or sharing our faith. Know the key scriptures listed below to share while convincing the unbeliever of God's love for them, and be ready to lead them to Christ if that opportunity comes to you. William Fay, in his book, _Share Jesus Without Fear_, calls these the...

Seven Share Scriptures.

2. Rom 3:23 - For all have sinned, and come short of the glory of God;

3. Rom 6:23 - For the wages of sin [is] death; but the gift of God [is] eternal life through Jesus Christ our Lord.

4. John 3:3 Jesus answered and said unto him, Verily, verily, I say unto thee, Except a man be born again, he cannot see the kingdom of God.

5. John 14:6 Jesus saith unto him, I am the way, the truth, and the life: no man cometh unto the Father, but by me.

6. Rom 10:9-10 [9]That if thou shalt confess with thy mouth the Lord Jesus, and shalt believe in thine heart that God hath raised him from the dead, thou shalt be saved. [10]For with the heart man believeth unto righteousness; and with the mouth confession is made unto salvation. [11]For the scripture saith, Whosoever believeth on him shall not be ashamed.

7. 2Co 5:15 - And [that] he died for all, that they which live should not henceforth live unto themselves, but unto him which died for them, and rose again.

8. Rev 3:20 - Behold, I stand at the door, and knock: if any man hear my voice, and open the door, I will come in to him, and will sup with him, and he with me.

After studying the scriptures above, write out your own testimony recounting what the Lord has done for you? Be prepared to be the Word of God to others as you share your living epistle.

Then list three (3) unchurched people who you will continuously pray for over the next month. Pray the following prayer concerning them:

Father in the name of Jesus' I pray that you would grant _____ the spirit of wisdom and revelation in the knowledge of you; the eyes of their understanding being enlightened that they may know what is the hope of your calling them; the riches of the glory of your inheritance in them; and the exceeding greatness of your power that is at work in them, that same power that raised Jesus from the dead.

I thank you that the glorious light of the gospel is shining in their heart and mind and dispelling the darkness that the god of this age has built up in them or in front of them. I thank you that your Light penetrates darkness and the darkness cannot comprehend or overcome it. I thank you that _____ is a believer and not a doubter and commits their life to you in Jesus' name. Amen.

Reflections

1. What has God done for you that you are most thankful for?

2. What has God delivered you from?

3. What scriptures are key to witnessing to someone?

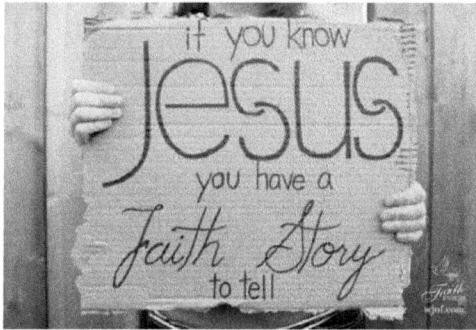

POST SCRIPT

This part of the Bible study has come to an end, but we must make sure our study of faith does not. If it means going back to lesson one of this study or picking up another faith-filled teaching, we can't let a day go by where we do not feed our faith. The enemy is waiting for us to go back to old habits and forget God's Word so he can reverse the newly developed habits of studying and meditating on the Word of God. If we don't continue in the Word, then satan can come in and like he did to Eve, cause us to question the Word of God then encourage us instead to believe in this world's ungodly standards.

We must also be committed to prayer, warring in the Spirit with the Word of God and instead of trying to fit quality time with God into our busy schedules - schedule our lives around our time with the Father.

God bless you and keep building your faith in the Word of the True and Living God. Jesus promised us in John 8:32 that we would know the Truth and the Truth would make us free!

Lisa

Footnotes

Lesson 1

[1]Vine's Complete Expository Dictionary of Old and New Testament Words: With Topical Index (Word Study) by W.E. Vine
[2]http://webstersdictionary1828.com/Dictionary/hope

Lesson 2

[1]Pierce, Larry. Outline of Biblical Usage, Online Bible
https://www.blueletterbible.org/lang/Lexicon/Lexicon.cfm?strongs=G4991&t=KJV

[2]Fortune, Don and Katie, Discover Your God-Given Gifts and Talents. Chosen Books; Revised, Expanded edition (November 1, 2009)

Lesson 3

[1] Hagin, Kenneth, Faith Bible Study, Harrison House Publishers, Tulsa, OK www.harrisonhouse.com
[2] https://www.medel.com/us/how-hearing-works/
[3]Vines Expository Dictionary of New Testament Words / Blueletterbible.com
https://www.blueletterbible.org/lang/Lexicon/Lexicon.cfm?strongs=G4487&t=KJV
[4]Copeland, Germaine. Prayers that Avail Much, Harrison House Publishers, Tulsa, OK.

Lesson 4

[1]https://clinicalpsychreading.blogspot.com/2016/04/why-is-us-suicide-rate-rising.html?m=1

Lesson 5

[1] Hagin, Kenneth E., Faith Bible Study, Harrison House Publishers, Tulsa, OK www.harrisonhouse.com

Lesson 6

[1]Strong, James. Strong's Exhaustive Concordance of the Bible. Abingdon Press, 1890. Print.

Lesson 7

Fay, William. Share Jesus Without Fear, Broadman & Holman Publishing; Reissue edition (June 1, 1999), Nashville, TN.

ABOUT THE AUTHOR

Minister Lisa C. Banks is an ordained Bible teacher who is passionate about sharing the Word of God which is empowered to set anyone who believes it free. She is the Christian Education director at Family Worship Center Church in Flint, MI where she has worn many hats through the years including Worship Leader, Children's Ministry Director, Financial Manager and Trustee.

Lisa is also a Certified Public Accountant (CPA) currently working as a Professor of Accounting and Entrepreneurship. She is a graduate of the University of Michigan Ross Business School, the University of Michigan-Flint School of Management, and Word of Life Bible Training Center.

Lisa has been married to her high school sweetheart, Rick, for 39 years and they are the proud parents of three amazing adult children, Brandon, Jamin and Briana.